Addressing the Challenging Behavior of Children with High-Functioning Autism/Asperger Syndrome in the Classroom

of related interest

Incorporating Social Goals in the Classroom
A Guide for Teachers and Parents of Children with High-Functioning
Autism and Asperger Syndrome
Rebecca A. Moyes
Foreword by Susan J. Moreno
ISBN 1 85302 967 X

Caring for a Child with Autism
A Practical Guide for Parents
Martine Ives and Nell Munro, National Autistic Society
ISBN 1 85302 996 3

Getting Services for your Child on the Autism Spectrum
De-Ann Hyatt-Foley and Matthew O. Foley
Foreword by Carol Gray
ISBN 1 85302 991 2

My Social Story Book
Carol Gray and Abbie Leigh White
Illustrated by Sean McAndrew
ISBN 1 85302 950 5

Asperger's Syndrome
A Guide for Parents and Professionals
Tony Attwood
Foreword by Lorna Wing
ISBN 1 85302 577 1

Pretending to be Normal
Living with Asperger's Syndrome
Liane Holliday Willey
Foreword by Tony Attwood
ISBN 1 85302 749 9

Asperger Syndrome in the Family
Redefining Normal
Liane Holliday Willey
Foreword by Pamela B. Tanguay
ISBN 1 85302 873 8

Addressing the Challenging Behavior of Children with High-Functioning Autism/Asperger Syndrome in the Classroom

A Guide for Teachers and Parents

Rebecca A. Moyes

Jessica Kingsley Publishers
London and Philadelphia

First published in the United Kingdom in 2002
by Jessica Kingsley Publishers Ltd
116 Pentonville Road
London N1 9JB, England
and
325 Chestnut Street
Philadelphia, PA 19106, USA

www.jkp.com

Copyright © 2002 Rebecca A. Moyes

Library of Congress Cataloging in Publication Data

Moyes, Rebecca A. (Rebecca Ann), 1960-
    Addressing the challenging behavior of children with high-functioning autism/Asperger syndrome in the classroom: a guide for teachers and parents / Rebecca A. Moyes.
    p.cm.
    Includes bibliographical references and index.
    ISBN 1-84310-719-8 (alk paper)
    1. Autistic children--Education. 2. Autistic children--Behavior modification. I. Title.

LC4717.5.M68 2002
371.94--dc21   2002021520

British Library Cataloguing in Publication Data
A CIP catalogue record for this book is available from the British Library

ISBN 1 84310 719 8

Printed and Bound in Great Britain by
Athenaeum Press, Gateshead, Tyne and Wear

Contents

Contents

I dedicate this book to my youngest child, Kiersten. Ever so patient, ever so kind, you have brought so much joy and happiness to our family. I am very blessed to have you as my daughter…my precious, beautiful, little girl.

Acknowledgements

These people deserve a special thank you for all their support of my efforts and of our special children:

- My son Chuck for his computer expertise and help with all the tables and charts in this book – he is a blessing to his mom.

- My husband, proofreader and facilitator of this project – his love and support continue to be my guiding star.

- My family, for their continued love and dedication.

- Nancy DePew, a kind shoulder and a wonderful resource to many parents of children with autism.

- Dondrea Blackwell, Diane Catterall, Pauline Springer, Debbie Strittmatter, and Karen Williams for their special contributions to this project.

- Debbie Leggens and her exceptional ability to step into the shoes of children with disabilities and fight for their needs.

And also:

- All the families who struggle with this diagnosis – may this book make your efforts a bit easier.

- All teachers of children with autism – may God grant you wisdom, patience and kindness.

- All individuals with autism – may you be blessed with hope and know that you truly are treasures in the lives that you touch.

Preface

I have always felt that there were two main arteries that seem to be the most difficult to navigate when we work with children with autism: how to address their social skills and what to do about problem behaviors. When I finished my first book, *Incorporating Social Goals in the Classroom – A Guide for Teachers and Parents of Children with High-Functioning Autism and Asperger Syndrome*, I realized that there was yet another that needed to be written. It is my deepest wish that you will find both books helpful.

As a former teacher, I am fortunate to be able to experience both the 'parent side' and the 'educator side.' I want parents to know that most teachers really do want to help our children; but they need training and support to be able to do an effective job. I also want teachers to know that our kids may be different from any other students you have had the pleasure to teach. Everything you may know about special needs children may not be enough. I also want teachers to know that they will probably never meet a student in their classroom as special and unique as a child with autism. If parents and teachers can learn to truly accept and appreciate the individuality of these children, they will be opening themselves up to a wonderful, enriching experience.

This book is not the answer to every behavior problem that ever existed in the field of autism. Its contents should not be used without careful consideration to the individual needs of each student. I am certain, however, that it will serve as a useful reference tool. You will be able to gather many helpful, practical ideas from its pages.

May your efforts be blessed, both parents and teachers, as you work together to establish solid supports for individuals with this diagnosis.

Rebecca A. Moyes, 2002

CHAPTER ONE

Traditional Approaches

For many children with autism, problems associated with behavior in the classroom can be expected. Indeed, behavioral differences are an important part of the diagnosis of autism and Asperger syndrome. The practice of including children with disabilities in typical classrooms, and in particular, children with autism, has not kept pace with providing training to school staff. If teachers felt competent in working with children with autism, they would be able to make the process of inclusion profitable for these children, as well as the typical students in their classrooms.

TRADITIONAL APPROACHES TO MANAGING POOR BEHAVIOR

Traditionally, the most common approaches that have been utilized to address problem behavior are aversives, restraints and/or behavior modification techniques.

Aversives

Aversives are defined as the use of negative reinforcers to interrupt or stop problem behaviors when they occur. Examples of frequently used aversives include reprimanding the child or removing enjoyable activities. However, in some places, other aversives used include squirts with water or other unpleasant substances, noxious-tasting materials and physical punishments (smacking, hitting).

> EXAMPLE I
> Ryan, when overwhelmed with his classwork, would frequently 'dump' all his papers off his desk. His teacher would then require Ryan to stand out in the hall by her door for ten minutes.
>
> Aversives can also be responses to behavior that, because of their dramatic effect, startle or scare the student into stopping the behavior.

> EXAMPLE II
> Peter had a particular sensitivity to loud noises. His teacher, in an effort to get Peter to comply, would often shout 'STOP THAT!' to get him to complete the task at hand.

Overcorrection, another type of aversive, is where the student is required to complete the appropriate behavior several times because he did not do it when asked, or because he continued negative behaviors when he was asked to stop.

> EXAMPLE
> Brad forgot to write his name on his homework paper. Since he did this quite frequently and reprimanding him did not seem to work, his teacher required Brad to stay in during recess time and write his name 100 times on a piece of paper.

It is important to understand that the use of aversives is a *response* to inappropriate behavior and should not be considered as a *preventative measure* for those types of behaviors.

Restraints

Restraints can be defined as techniques, appliances, etc. that restrain or 'hold back' a student from doing something which is dangerous to him/herself or others. Restraints might also be used to help secure attention, such as the use of seatbelts in classroom chairs.

EXAMPLE I

Michael, when stressed, would frequently begin to hit or kick his peers. His teacher, in an effort to calm him down, would often grab him, force his hands down and wrap her arms around his torso until he could contain himself.

EXAMPLE II

Sarah rode a special mini-van to school. She would often leave her seat and bother the other children or the driver. Finally, a seatbelt was installed in her seat. Sarah was buckled in each day so that she could not disturb the other individuals on the van.

EXAMPLE III

Robert would have several episodes a day where he would begin to bang his head hard on his desk. Staff could not discover any responses to this behavior that stopped the head banging. His school ordered a special helmet for Robert to wear that prevented him from inflicting injury to himself when he banged his head. This did not stop the frequency of this behavior, but prevented Robert from injuring himself.

Behavior modification

Another way to manage behavior is through behavior modification – the use of a collection of techniques that are assembled to increase the number of desirable behaviors and decrease or 'extinguish' the number of undesirable behaviors. Behavior modification only takes into consideration those behaviors that are observable and measurable. Behaviorists do not attempt to discover the reasons or causes for such behavior. 'Targeted behaviors' are broken down into tiny pieces of mastery that lead to the targeted behaviors. The tiny pieces are taught first and rewarded until they are mastered. Punishments (reprimands, withdrawal of privileges or favorite objects, time outs, and/or overcorrections) are used to decrease the number of undesirable behaviors, as are restraints and aversives. Generalizing the student's responses so that they are appropriate in other settings and with other teachers may also have to be taught.

EXAMPLE I

Lisa frequently flapped her hands. Her teacher used overcorrection to stop this behavior. Lisa's teacher would place her hands in her lap and then on her desk ten times every time Lisa flapped. She would reprimand Lisa with a statement: 'No flapping!' When Lisa did not flap for intervals of 15 minutes, she received a pretzel stick, her favorite food reward.

EXAMPLE II

Robert's teacher was trying to teach him to attend to completing a task. First, she had to teach him to sit in a chair. Then Robert had to learn to stay seated in the chair for 15 minutes. Robert also had to learn to look into his teacher's eyes. All of the above had to be taught and rewarded first before he could begin to attend to completing a task.

EXAMPLE III

Lisa's kindergarten teacher was trying to encourage her to help clean up the toys. Lisa would put one or two toys away and then wander off while the other children in the class completed the task. The teacher was instructed by a behavior therapist to reward Lisa as soon as she helped with one or two toys, rather than waiting for her to put them all away. Lisa's teacher was *shaping* her behavior by reinforcing approximations of the desired behavior.

Again, it is important to note that although behavior modification is a commonly used approach for handling problem behavior, it does not take into consideration the *reason* for such behavior. For instance, if a student is exhibiting self-stimulatory behavior because he is stressed, overcorrection may result in the student replacing one self-stimulatory behavior with another.

IS THERE ANOTHER WAY TO ADDRESS BEHAVIOR PROBLEMS?

> Communication difficulties constitute one of the principal deficit areas in the syndrome of autism. Behavioral problems and atypical social skills development are other characteristics of this disorder. There is increasing professional acknowledgement of the relationship between the communication difficulty experienced by children (i.e. with autism) and the number of behavioral problems they may display. (Hodgdon 1995, p.265)

The amount of time that it takes to prepare how a teacher will respond to negative behaviors can be overwhelming. Teachers and staff may constantly feel as if they are 'on edge' waiting for the behavior to occur and then worrying if their responses are going to be effective. The use of a systematic approach to solving behavior problems that strongly takes into consideration *the reason for why the behavior is occurring* and builds the communication bridge to help prevent those problem behaviors can be far less frustrating.

The purpose of this book is to present such an approach. It begins with the use of a formal behavior support plan (Appendix 1.1). This plan takes into consideration what the student may be thinking and/or feeling as a reason for why his behavior is occurring. Creating environmental supports for problem behaviors and incorporating specific teaching strategies are one phase of this approach. The other phase is to teach students with autism the skills they are lacking so that they might then be able to behave appropriately.

As teachers and parents, we frequently acknowledge the need to teach our children to 'own' their behaviors. However, we must also recognize the need to be able to provide our children with meaningful strategies to help them accomplish this in their home, community and school environments.

APPENDIX 1.1

Behavioral Support Plan

Student Name:_____Date: _____

Define the problem behavior and why it is important to change:

Hypothesis regarding the problem behavior:

Identified skill to be taught to reduce problem behavior:

Antecedent strategies to put in place to prevent behavior:

Hierarchy of consequential strategies to use when behavior occurs:

Reward system for good behavior:

Methods and dates of data collection for evaluation:

CHAPTER TWO

Adopting a Team Approach to Writing a Behavioral Support Plan

Often, teachers and parents struggle with not only how to address problem behaviors, but when to address them. They may differ on what behaviors need to be tackled and/or what methods should be used to control them. As we will see in Chapter 3, the process of effectively addressing challenging behaviors comes from understanding why they are occurring. As mentioned previously, we spend many hours as educators and parents planning out possible responses to inappropriate behavior. Very little time is spent on putting preparations in place to prevent problem behavior or discovering why it may be occurring. Looking at negative behaviors as a form of communication (sophisticated or not, appropriate or not) will help us to decide what to do to help reduce the number of times these behaviors occur. In Chapter 3, we will focus on possible reasons for poor behavior. In this chapter, however, we will learn to observe behaviors using a nonjudgmental approach. We will learn to gather information as a team and analyze it systematically – free from the emotions that often cloud our lens. Gathering information from observation is the first step in developing a positive behavior support plan (Appendix 2.1).

DECIDING WHETHER OR NOT TO ADDRESS PROBLEM BEHAVIORS

This author has frequently been approached by parents who describe their child's behavior in the classroom. They go on to say that the teacher feels that certain things their child does are distracting and they want the behavior to stop. The parents, however, may feel that even if the behaviors are odd, the child should be allowed to continue them if he/she is not causing harm. For instance, one family reported that their son Mark would frequently flick his fingers in front of his face at his desk during class. His teacher insisted that this behavior impeded his ability to pay attention. The parents, however, felt that it was vital for their child to be able to de-stress as it helped him to relax so he would not experience sensory overload.

Generally parents want teachers to be more flexible in allowing certain behaviors because they may be serving a purpose for the child (as we will see in Chapter 3). It doesn't seem fair to punish a child for being different, or for displaying symptoms of his/her disability. On the flip side, however, teachers worry about granting favors to one student, but not another. Order must be kept; an environment conducive to learning must be maintained. What if everyone were to begin flicking their fingers? If we want the child with autism to experience inclusion and meet with success, then isn't he/she going to have to be able to adapt his/her behavior to promote inclusion? As we have seen by the above example, coming to a planning table as parents and teachers for behavior management issues can sometimes be quite difficult.

Education law (Individuals with Disabilities Education Act, IDEA 1999) suggests a basic rule of thumb: the types of behaviors that need to be addressed are those that interfere with the student's or that of the other students' ability to learn. If Mark is able to keep his attention and maintain a C grade or better and still flick his fingers when he needs to, then it appears that, according to the first part of the above rule of thumb, Mark's behavior would not need to be addressed. However, if

Mark's flicking makes other students complain or distracts his teacher from her presentation, then certainly, we will need to stop this behavior. It is also important to note that Mark's behavior may not be bothersome on some days or to some teachers, but on other days and to other teachers it might.

This author, if asked to participate in a meeting concerning Mark's behavior on this particular issue, would ask *how often* the behavior is occurring and take into consideration *the possible reasons why Mark needs to flick his fingers.* Is there anything we can do for Mark that would decrease the desire to engage in this behavior? If flicking his fingers helps Mark to relax but this is bothersome to his classmates and teacher, perhaps we could find a more socially acceptable and less distracting way for him to do this. For instance, could Mark be provided with a squeeze ball instead? Could we build some vigorous exercise into his school routine to help relieve stress? Could we call upon the expertise of an occupational therapist to offer some suggestions on ways to manage sensory overload? Indeed, are we absolutely sure that he is flicking his fingers because he has sensory overload?

When parents and educators come to the table to discuss problem behaviors, it is important to adopt a *team approach.* The decisions of the team must come about after a systematic approach to looking at the behavior. Once methods are put in place to address this behavior, they must be adopted and used by everyone who works with the student. Just as parents must be in agreement with the way they handle behavior problems at home, parents and teachers must also be in agreement with the way they are handled at school. If the student's plan is to be effective for him/her, it must be adopted and supported by everyone who works with him/her.

Several of the student's teachers should serve as team members. The student's parents should also be included. In addition, an occupational therapist, language therapist, and someone familiar with autism should hold seats on the team. These people bring an expertise to the table that may prove beneficial. The student might also be able to offer insight.

GATHERING INFORMATION

Often, it is useful for teachers and parents to appoint a team member to be the record-keeper. This person should be someone on the team who is willing to act as a neutral party and report all information in an unbiased format. So that each party feels they have a chance to input what they want to share, a form can be used to gather this data. An example, the Gathering of Information Form for Behavioral Assessment, is presented in Appendix 2.1. This form could be used to collect information prior to observation. The record-keeper distributes this form to each party in the group and asks that it be returned and completed by a specified date. From this information, he/she will organize the data so that the form is summarized with every participant's input. This will help focus the group's attention on the behaviors that appear to be most troublesome, what things have been tried in the past, and identify some possible hypotheses (reasons) for the behavior.

Throughout this book, we will use a case study of Scott Smith, a 9-year-old fourth grade student with autism, and continue to build a behavior support plan for him at the end of each chapter. Scott is displaying aggressive tendencies in his school environment. He will frequently hit his classmates when he is frustrated or angry. On occasion, he also has crying spells and yells out in class.

It is suggested that no more than two or three behaviors be formally addressed in a behavior support plan so that the student and staff are not overwhelmed. On the Gathering of Information form, four problem behaviors are identified to ensure that the 'top three' can be addressed. If the behaviors are believed by the team to be a direct result of the same hypothesis, then only one form will be needed. However, if the behaviors have different suspected causes, then a separate form will be needed for each behavior that will be addressed.

Reinforcers that have worked for parents or for some teachers should be identified and shared with the other team members. The same holds true for those that did not work – we certainly would not want to waste time using things that have been tried and have not been helpful. This procedure also applies to consequences. Questions #4 and #5 are important because they help the team members to begin focusing on looking at the behavior as a form of communication.

Once the information has all been gathered via a form, the record-keeper can begin to assemble the Gathering of Information Summary Report for the team (Appendix 2.3). The author suggests that for each question, a list should be made from the data gathered by each individual form and tallies kept to keep track of participant responses.

For Question #1: '*What four behaviors of the student do you find most troubling to work with?*', the method shown in Figure 2.1 could be used to organize participant data. This will not only give the team a good indication of the three most troublesome behaviors, but also enable everyone to see what other behavior problems may exist.

Spinning pencils	/ /
Unorganized	/
Hitting and pushing	/ / / / /
Crying spells	/ / /
Yelling out	/ / / / /

Summary: the three most troublesome behaviors are hitting and pushing, yelling out and crying spells.

Figure 2.1 Summary of troublesome behaviors

For Question #2: '*Describe the consequences you have tried that have worked or not worked when the behavior has occurred (verbal warnings, time-outs, etc.)*', a chart can be made to keep track of these responses (Figure 2.2). The same method should be used for Question #3.

	Worked	Not Worked
Time-outs	/	
Losing recess		/
Verbal warning	/ / /	
Loss of computer time	/ / / /	

Summary: verbal warnings and loss of computer time work best, time-outs also work, losing recess does not.

Figure 2.2 Consequences that have worked or not worked

For Question #4, comments should be examined to see if there is a possible thread, and then they too should be summarized: 'Three people on the team felt that Scott's behaviors surfaced more during reading time,' or 'two people felt that Scott exhibited aggression most during art class.'

Lastly for Question #5, personal information should be included in the summary report, but the name of the individual who wrote it should not be added to keep the report unbiased. A copy of the Gathering of Information Summary Report (Appendix 2.3) should be provided for each team member and reviewed with them. Sometimes this is done by merely distributing the report to team members rather than holding a meeting. The disadvantage of this method is that an opportunity is missed to gather additional data that team members might share with the group. More importantly, if parents are to feel supportive of the efforts of staff to understand their child, seeing how the information was gathered, collected, and reported factually may help them to have confidence that their child is not being singled out by staff for punishment.

OBSERVATION

The Observation of Student Behavior Form (Appendix 2.2) is used in the next step of the process of developing a behavior support plan. The student is now observed during various parts of the school day, as unobtrusively as possible, by team members. The author would like to explain that it is crucial that only the top three problem behaviors should be observed at this point. For this reason, the three most troublesome behaviors identified from the Gathering of Information Summary Report should be written at the top of this form to help team members focus on looking at only those behaviors.

As mentioned previously, it is helpful to have someone who is familiar with autism participate in the observation process and/or serve on the team because often he/she has witnessed many of the behaviors these children may display and can help the team identify why they might be occurring. Each team member should conduct at least three observations across two weeks at various times of the day. Parents should also be invited to complete three observations if possible as well. This will build trust and help them to feel as if they are active participants in the process of finding a solution to the problem behaviors. This process should not be rushed, as the observations need to show the behavior in its truest fashion. In some circumstances, for instance, when behaviors are escalating, school staff may try to rush through the observations and conclude them in a day or so. It is important to refrain from doing this, as it will only result in a plan that does not work for the student.

If no negative behaviors are observed during the time that the child is being observed, then only the top of the form is completed. Such information is also useful to know as it helps to show what periods of the day are not providing the student with problems and in what areas he is showing positive behaviors.

After three observation forms have been completed by each team member, again the record-keeper will produce an Observation Report summarizing the findings of the team for each team member (Appendix 2.4). The clock time and schedule time of each negative behavior also need to be noted and tallied. (For instance, Scott had two incidents of aggression in reading class between 10 and 10:45 am, one while moving to art class, and two in art class between 10:48 and 11:30 am. He also cried immediately after recess at 1:00pm.) It is important to differentiate clock time from schedule time. For example, not only did Scott have six problems with aggression and crying in the span of three hours, but they all occurred during reading and art, or in moving from one area to another. (Someone familiar with autism might begin to think that perhaps he was on 'overload' in reading and art, and/or perhaps the transition to the next class was difficult for him.) It is also recommended that the frequency of each behavior be presented in graph form for the team.

When the report is prepared, the record-keeper should share with the team all the results for Question #7: '*Do you have any theories as to why the behavior occurred?*' Everyone's view as to what the *hypothesis* or reason for the behavior should be considered. The Observation Report should be shared in a team meeting as well to gain further input from the various viewpoints.

For parents, knowing that the school is considering the individual problems of the student and having a say in the process of developing a behavior support plan will build confidence that what the team is doing is right for their son or daughter. If parents feel that their child is understood and his/her behaviors are being addressed appropriately, they will be more likely to accept the adoption of the plan and support it. This will lend more consistency for the child in both his/her home/school environments and enable families to feel that they are active partners in the education of their child with autism.

APPENDIX 2.1

Gathering of Information Form
For Behavioral Assessment

Your name:_____Name of student:_____

Your relationship to student: _____

1. What four behaviors of the student do you find most troubling to work with?

    (a) _____

    (b) _____

    (c) _____

    (d) _____

2. Describe the consequences you have tried that have worked or not worked when the behavior has occurred (verbal warnings, time-outs, etc.):

    (a) _____

    (b) _____

    (c) _____

3. What reinforcers have you tried this past year to encourage positive behavior?

    (a) _____

    (b) _____

    (c) _____

4.   Are there any situations that generally happen before inappropriate behaviors are exhibited (for instance, the student is asked to complete math worksheets, or the student is asked to go to music class, or the student is asked to wait in line)?

_____

_____

_____

_____

5.   Please provide at the bottom and/or on the back, any additional information you want to share for this assessment or any personal feelings or reactions you have about the student's behavior and his/her relationship with you:

_____

_____

_____

_____

APPENDIX 2.2

Observation of Student Behavior Form

Name of observer: _____ Relationship to student: _____

Name of student: _____

Date of observation: _____

Three behaviors to be observed: _____

1.   Time of observation (please include clock time, and also a description of the student's schedule at that time: for instance, 12:00 noon, lunchtime):

_____

2.   If the child exhibited problem behavior, what did he or she do that was troublesome?

_____

_____

3.   If the child did not exhibit problem behavior, what positive behaviors did you observe?

_____

_____

4.   Describe, as completely as you can, what you observed immediately prior to the problem behavior (i.e. What was going on in the classroom? What was the child doing? Were there any provocations? Did the child provide any distress signals?):

_____

_____

_____

5.   How was the problem behavior handled?

_____

_____

6.   How did the student respond?

_____

_____

7.   Do you have any theories as to why the behavior occurred?

_____

_____

_____

APPENDIX 2.3

Gathering of Information Summary Report
Scott Smith
January 24, 2002

Introduction: There were nine Gathering of Information forms that were collected. These were obtained from Scott's regular education classroom teachers; his teacher assistant; his learning support teacher; his music, art and physical education teacher; his occupational therapist and his speech/language therapist. His mother and his father also completed one.

Four behaviors identified: The team identified that the four behaviors that were most troublesome (in order of worst to least severe) included hitting and pushing, yelling out, crying spells, and spinning pencils [see Figure 2.1]. The team will address hitting and pushing, yelling out and crying spells as the three most troublesome behaviors.

Consequences tried: The team identified the most effective consequence is when Scott loses computer time. Verbal warnings also work, but not as well [see Figure 2.2].

Positive reinforcers tried: The team only identified verbal praise as a positive reinforcer that has been tried. Some team members felt that it was useful sometimes, but not all times.

Precursors to problem behavior: The team identified several precursors to problem behaviors. Scott's classroom teacher and his teacher assistant felt that behaviors occurred when he was asked to complete challenging reading work; for instance, when he was asked to do comprehension papers. His art teacher said that Scott seems to be upset the moment he walks in her class and appears disoriented and inattentive.

She also noticed that he would frequently become aggressive when he was asked to do certain types of projects. Scott's learning support teacher felt that his frustration tolerance was very low when she worked on his reading papers with him. His physical education teacher and music teacher said that although Scott sometimes appeared 'disorganised' at the beginning of class, he generally did not act out in those classes. His occupational therapist said that her session was first thing in the morning, and although it took a few minutes to get Scott 'settled down,' he didn't seem to have behaviors for her. The speech therapist also remarked that it was the same for her. His mother and father observed Scott during recess and felt that moving from recess to his next class was troublesome for Scott, as he appeared agitated and confused.

Additional information shared: Several team members felt that Scott was a pleasant child with a good sense of humor. He has a good relationship with his teachers. He also has two friends, Robert and Matthew, whom he plays with on the playground. His parents described that he has a real 'passion' for airplanes and airplane-related items. His classroom teacher shared that she feels the reading work in his grade level is too hard from him. His classroom assistant feels that changes are difficult for Scott and that he needs more structure to his day. He also does not like to be around a certain boy in his class (Ryan) who tends to 'invade his space' too much.

Theories for the behavior: Several team members felt that Scott's reading work was too hard for him. They felt his work needed to be modified or that he needed additional support in this area. His parents and occupational therapist felt that Scott also had issues with sensory problems – he needed his own space and did not tolerate individuals who touched him. His parents and classroom assistant felt that transitions were also difficult for Scott.

APPENDIX 2.4

Summary of Observation Forms
Scott Smith
February 5, 2002

Three behaviors that were observed:

Hitting and pushing, yelling out, and crying spells.

Summary of observations:

The team completed 27 observations across two weeks from January 21 to February 1 at various times during Scott's school day.

Clock time/schedule time of troublesome behaviors observed:

During the two-week span, there were three incidents of aggression in reading class from 10–10:45 am, one incident while Scott was moving to art class at 10:46 am and two in art class between 10:48 and 11:30 am. Scott also exhibited one crying spell and one yelling out in reading class connected with the above incidents. In another incident, he cried and yelled at 1:00 pm when he was moving from recess back to his classroom.

What troublesome behaviors were observed? What happened immediately before they occurred? How was the behavior handled? How did the student respond?

In the first incident of aggression, Monday, January 21, Scott was having trouble completing a comprehension worksheet in reading. He began to look disturbed, and his movements became more agitated. He slammed his fist on his desk and threw the paper on the floor. His classroom assistant attempted to pick it up and put it back on his desk, and Scott reached over to hit her. She avoided the hit by backing up. She said in an angry tone, 'No hitting Scott!' Scott began to cry quietly with his hand over his eyes to 'shield' them from his peers and teachers. After about 15 minutes, the class was over and the students lined up for art class. Scott took a spot in the back of the line and appeared to be more calm.

In the second incident of aggression, also in reading, on Tuesday, January 22, Scott yelled out in a loud voice, 'Where are we?' to his teacher. A peer sitting beside Scott (Rachel) tried to redirect him to a page in the book by leaning in close to him and pointing her finger to the spot where the class was. Suddenly, Scott reached over and angrily punched her in the arm. Again, his classroom teacher and teacher's aide both gave him a strong verbal prompt, 'No hitting Scott!' His teacher's aide told Scott that he would lose his computer time for hitting Rachel explaining: 'Rachel was trying to help you find your place!' Scott did appear somewhat remorseful, though he didn't offer an apology. His face was red, and again, he shielded his eyes from his class but did not appear to be crying. The class resumed their work, and there were no further incidents that day.

There was no reading class on Wednesday, January 23, due to an assembly. Scott participated well and seemed to enjoy himself in the assembly, though he was observed sitting apart from the group as they sat cross-legged on the floor.

The third incident of aggression on Thursday, January 24, also in reading, occurred when Scott was completing a reading test. His face became red, his movements became agitated, and then he crumpled the test and threw it on the floor. He then attempted to stop his neighbor from taking her test by grabbing her arm. His classroom aide removed Scott from the room, and the observer was not able to see what happened at this point.

Scott also exhibited an act of aggression while moving to art class. Scott was placed in the middle of the line by his classroom assistant and another student, Ryan, was in line behind him. Ryan reached his hands around Scott's neck from behind. Scott reacted violently, turned around and punched him in the stomach. Scott then attempted to move to the back of the line. His aide prompted him to remain where he was, but Scott was clearly disturbed. He did manage to maintain his spot in line and move to art class without further incident.

During art class that same day, Scott hit his classroom assistant when she attempted to provide him with a wet paper towel. Scott had made a substantial mess with his glue as he attempted to glue small pieces of colored paper onto another piece of paper. He was becoming distressed because his hands were sticky. His classroom teacher and his classroom assistant asked Scott to go into the hall with them. They talked with him there, but the observer was not able to see this. Scott came back into the room, visibly upset, but continued his work. He lost his computer time for that day as a result of his behavior. There were no further incidents that day.

On Thursday, January 31, another incident in art occurred when Scott had trouble using his scissors and a peer (Jarrot) attempted to help him. Scott angrily pushed the peer away. His assistant again told Scott that Jarrot was only trying to help and asked him to apologize to Jarrot. Scott did apologize, with his head down and his face red. There was also a crying spell and a 'yelling out' shortly after recess on Monday, January 28. When Scott heard the bell that signals the end of recess, he shouted, 'I hate that bell!' and began to cry. His assistant prompted him to get in line to enter the building. Scott continued to cry and look agitated. Once inside and his class began, Scott seemed to calm down.

What positive behaviors were exhibited?

During all of his other subjects, Scott appears to be exhibiting positive behavior. He sits quietly, raises his hand when he wants to share or answer a question, smiles at his peers, and appears for the most part to be 'part of the group.' He does occasionally need vocal prompting to get organized or to maintain his attention, but he responds well to these prompts. He has a good relationship with his teachers and most of the peers in his class. He also joins in at recess time in peer games. During lunchtime, several observers noticed him smiling and chatting with peers. He prefers to take a seat at the end of the table but still maintains some conversations with those around him.

Theories for behavior:

There were several theories that became apparent as a result of the observations. His occupational therapist felt that Scott needed more work in the development of his fine motor skills. He disliked messy projects and cutting was difficult for him. His art teacher agreed with this. His parents felt that the sensory experience of glue and having people 'in his space' also bothered him and caused him to overreact. His classroom assistant felt that at times, Scott was embarrassed when she would intervene to help him. She felt that he still needed prompting but also was craving more independence. She also pointed out that transitions were difficult for him and that Scott performed better when he knew what was happening next. She noticed that Mondays appeared to be hard for Scott. Scott's classroom teacher and learning support teacher felt that his reading work was too difficult for him and needed to be modified.

CHAPTER THREE

What Causes Misbehavior in Children with Autism?

Forming a Hypothesis

The first step to addressing problem behavior is to discover a hypothesis or reason for the behavior. In order to do this, we need to look at problem behavior as a form of communication. If we can discover the reasons for poor behavior, then we can certainly apply some meaningful strategies to help prevent it.

As teachers, when troublesome behavior occurs, we should ask ourselves the following questions: What happened to the student prior to the misbehavior? Did the behavior occur 'out of the blue' or were there any warning signs? Who was with or near the child when the behavior occurred? What skills does the student lack that would enable him to refrain from using the behavior? Is the student using the behavior to *get* something or *escape* something? Playing detective can certainly help us discover reasons for problem behaviors that we may not have considered. Even so, we may not be able to identify these 'triggers,' unless we have an understanding of the core deficits of children with autism.

This chapter will provide some possible reasons (hypotheses) for problem behavior in children with autism (Figure 3.1). Chapter 4 will help us to address them.

- Receptive language and language processing difficulties
- Social language difficulties
- Social behavior problems
- Sensory processing differences
- Problems handling transitions and change
- Problems with self-esteem and/or depression
- Weakness in organizational skills and task sequencing
- Academic and/or athletic skill deficits
- Difficulty managing stress and anxiety
- Attention problems

Figure 3.1 Hypotheses for problem behavior in children with Autism

LANGUAGE PROCESSING AND RECEPTIVE LANGUAGE DIFFICULTIES

Processing language involves taking in the speech sounds that one hears and converting them into patterns for understanding. Children with receptive language difficulties and language processing problems may not be attentive in periods where teachers are lecturing and/or they may not be able to follow long strands of directions. When given a task to complete, they may forget what they were asked to do or only be able to complete a few steps.

EXAMPLE I

Joshua, a child with autism, was listening to the teacher's instructions. There were five things that he had to remember to do to complete a worksheet. Joshua accomplished the first three directives but left out the next two. Consequently, he received a poor grade on his worksheet and became very angry and kicked the child sitting across from him.

EXAMPLE II

Brad was given a verbal list by his teacher of his homework assignments for the evening. All the other children had packed their bookbags and were ready for the bus. Brad was the last child to be ready. That night, his mother discovered that he had forgotten two of the books he needed for homework. When she discussed this with her son, he became tearful and called himself 'stupid.'

EXAMPLE III

Michael was inattentive to his teacher as she discussed at length the various battles of World War II. He became fidgety in his seat. When his aide prompted him to pay attention, he angrily threw his book on the floor.

Echolalia

Children with autism may also use echolalia, the repetition of speech or phrases, to help them process what they heard. They may not respond to questions or may take unusually long to provide answers to the same. Finally, if they are able to provide answers, the answers may be unrelated to the actual questions asked.

Echolalia may be used by the student for various reasons. As Barry Prizant has shown in his studies of the communicative intent of echolalia (Prizant and Duchan 1981), the child repeats phrases or speech that he has previously heard in an attempt to express a thought, or to ask for help.

EXAMPLE IV

One 8-year-old with Asperger Syndrome approached his teacher during recess and said, 'There's a crisis in aisle four!' Apparently, he had heard this phrase on television and was trying to explain to her that there was a fight breaking out between two other students.

In other instances, echolalia may be used as a calming technique for the child.

> EXAMPLE V
>
> A 6-year-old child with autism was becoming anxious in his kindergarten classroom during a class party when things were noisy and unstructured. He approached his aide and said, 'Take a deep breath now!' with an anxious face. This child was attempting to communicate to his teacher his stress by referring to a phrase that his parents sometimes used when they wanted him to try to calm himself down.

Echolalia may be a precursor to more normal speech and is often serving a communicative function for the child so it is important that it not be extinguished. It is not hard to see that when a child has difficulty with receptive language, he may also have trouble responding appropriately with his behavior. He may appear noncompliant, when in fact he didn't understand what he was asked to do. He may be experiencing stress when he is bombarded with speech that is too complex for his understanding, or he may only be able to process bits and pieces. An individual with autism once compared his understanding of speech to that of the volume knob of a radio being turned repetitively back and forth – he could only understand selected portions of communication. This may cause the individual to respond inappropriately with anger or demonstrate frustration.

In addition, it is also important to note that a child's *expressive language* may be more advanced than his *receptive language*. Do not assume that because a child seems to be using a fluent level of speech that he is able to *process* speech at this same level.

SOCIAL LANGUAGE DIFFICULTIES

Children with autism spectrum disorders have difficulty with social language, or *pragmatic* language. They may not understand how to begin a conversation, maintain the topic of conversation, use modulation in their voices and/or read the same in others. These are the social niceties that make us adept in communication. Children with autism may also use words or phrases in unusual ways.

> EXAMPLE I
> A ten-year-old boy with high-functioning autism thoroughly enjoyed his dinner of roast beef and asked his mother if he could have some more *game*. It took several minutes before his mother understood what he was referring to. [meat] (Moyes 2001, p.25)

> EXAMPLE II
> An 8-year-old child with autism had a fascination with trees. He often would compare certain types of trees to people. Once he was angry at his mother and told her she was nothing but an 'old willow.'

Children with autism may also be literal in their understanding of spoken language and may react in odd ways because of this.

> EXAMPLE III
> Bryan, a student with autism, was well known for his ability to follow and police the school rules. One day Bryan became quite ill in class and had a significant fever. He felt that he would break the 'no interrupting' rule if he raised his hand to inform his teacher. Much later, his teacher discovered that Bryan was ill when he wrote on his afternoon worksheet, 'I am in need of serious medical attention.'

Students with this diagnosis may be blunt or socially inappropriate with others. They may have difficulty maintaining eye contact and not be able to read cues when they are boring someone with their conversations. It is easy to see how problems with peers and teachers can come about because of social language differences.

EXAMPLE IV

A sixth-grade student had accrued a massive amount of information about weather patterns. He would frequently approach his peers and begin to discuss cloud formations or barometric readings, despite the fact that his peers were not interested and it was not an appropriate time.

SOCIAL BEHAVIOR PROBLEMS

Children with autism may have trouble taking on another's perspective. Participating in pretend play and using imitative skills are difficult for many of these individuals. It is often hard for them to enter into play with other children, maintain that play, and be appropriate. Indeed, far after other children have mastered the rules of simple childhood games (kickball, dodgeball, baseball), these children may not understand what is expected of them in team sports. Even understanding basic turn taking may ellude them.

EXAMPLE I

At recess, Johnny, a child with autism, frequently paces around the perimeter of the play area and acts as if he doesn't know what to do. At other times, he attempts to play for a minute or two with someone and then walks off.

EXAMPLE II

Michelle, a 7-year-old child with autism, becomes very upset when she feels that others are not understanding the rules of a game or activity. She resorts to biting everyone within easy distance of herself.

Children with this diagnosis may also have difficulty reading nonverbal cues and gestures, judging proper body distance, deciphering facial expressions and body language. Sometimes they cannot express their anger appropriately. When they are anxious or stressed, they may not be able to let others know how they are feeling and may react violently or aggressively. They also have trouble reading social situations (such as friendly vs. mean-spirited teasing) and may respond inappropriately because of this.

> EXAMPLE III
> One pre-adolescent boy with autism could not understand that children may tease each other in fun. He has been taught that teasing is wrong. Some of this may be due to his literal interpretation of this social rule and that, to him, no gray areas can exist. When he is teased, even if it is friendly teasing, he overreacts, yells and sometimes hits the offender.

SENSORY PROCESSING DIFFERENCES

> Sensory integration is the neurological process that organizes sensation from one's own body and from the environment and makes it possible to use the body effectively within the environment. (Ayers 1989, p.11)

A child with disorganized sensory processing may exhibit difficulty in learning as well as display maladaptive behaviors. Children with sensory problems may display underreaction to certain stimuli or overreaction to the same. As an example, a child with extreme taste preferences may crave a certain food or avoid it altogether.

Behaviors in various types of classrooms can arise from sensory processing difficulties. A child with visual perception deficits may exhibit problems in physical education class. He may not be able to judge distances or anticipate a ball being thrown in his direction. This may impact his behavior with poor self-confidence or low self-esteem when the other children begin to recognize his ineptness and bring it to his attention. A child with spatial problems may be distracted by objects hanging from the ceiling or lose his way in the hallways. If a student with autism has tactile problems, he may dislike messy art projects, not be able to maintain a grasp on a pencil and become tired while completing lengthy writing assignments. He may overreact when he is touched a certain way. A child with proprioceptive problems (being able to judge one's position in space) may have poor motor planning, be a messy eater, refrain from using playground equipment and/or have difficulty sitting in a chair. Vestibular differences (those involving balance) may cause a child to head bang, become nauseous with movement or actually crave spinning or rocking motions. Autistic adults share with us their problems with their sense of vision and sound.

> EXAMPLE I
> Temple Grandin (1995, p.74) reports that 'fluorescent lighting causes severe problems for many autistic people because they can see a 60-cycle flicker. Household electricity turns on and off 60 times each second, and some autistic people see this.'

Families also report how these problems can affect their children with autism.

> EXAMPLE II
> One mother reports that her son is deathly afraid of Warner Brother's Tweety character and suspects that it has something to do with the sound of his voice.

PROBLEMS HANDLING TRANSITIONS AND CHANGE

Many students with autism crave routine. Because of their sensory processing issues and/or their communication difficulties, they want to be comfortable in their environment and know what is expected of them. At a conference (Pittsburgh, Pennsylvania 2001), Dr Tony Attwood reported that an adult with autism was once asked what his definition of hell was like. The man replied, 'Change.' Change is indeed difficult for many individuals with autism. When students with autism are suddenly asked, without warning, to move on to a new task or new environment, they may become very anxious. This change in routine may also raise their level of anxiety and lower their ability to concentrate. These students may resist the change by complaining or resist with their behavior by becoming aggressive or defiant. They may tantrum or become agitated. Too many unexpected changes in the day may cause them to be overwhelmed and experience a 'melt-down.'

EXAMPLE I
Seven-year-old Larry, after getting into line to go to art class, all at once jumped out of his place and ran from the room.

EXAMPLE II
Nine-year-old Rose, when moving from recess back to her classroom, would frequently hide under the coat of her teacher aide. When they arrived at the classroom door, she would fall to the floor and cry.

The traditional way of moving from class to class is in a line. Sometimes, the sensory difficulties are too much for the child. At other times coping with the transition and the sensory problems together produce problems. The teacher can plan for transitions by using many of the suggestions in Chapter 4.

PROBLEMS WITH SELF-ESTEEM AND/OR DEPRESSION

Many children with autism, especially the children who are higher functioning, become keenly aware of their differences as they approach grade three or four (and sometimes even sooner). For some children with autism, their difficulties at school become so overwhelming that they cannot see their positive qualities at all. As we have seen in the example where the boy forgot to bring home his textbooks, when adults and other children point out their deficits, glimmers of depression or anger may surface. No one can 'beat themselves up' more than the child him/herself who is experiencing low self-esteem.

Often times, teacher aides or therapeutic staff personnel are assigned to prompt children with autism throughout their school day. These children may certainly have need for such help. However, they may also be aware that other children do not have these supports, which may cause them some embarrassment. They may become mean to their support personnel or refuse to take direction from these staff members. The children may refuse to join in tasks or avoid work that makes them feel inadequate (physical education, recess games, math or reading work, art class). Teachers may notice an explosion of negative behaviors when they are asked to do these types of activities.

> EXAMPLE I
> Michael participated in a social skills camp for children with autism. When he was made to participate in a game, he would angrily throw the ball far from the play area, or spit on it. His therapist had resorted to 'timing' him with a timer to ensure that he participated for at least ten minutes. Michael, on one occasion, became enraged when his ten minutes had not lapsed and threw the timer.

> EXAMPLE II
> Eight-year-old Allison refuses to join in many of the activities at girlscout meetings. Frustrated, her mother will frequently prompt her to participate. Allison will usually reply, 'I can't do that; I don't know how.' Often, when her mother tries to show her how to do the activity, Allison will continue to express her unwillingness to try.

Often times these children may need professional help to enable them to deal with their feelings of inadequacy and low self-esteem. Sometimes, this leads to a prescription for antidepressants or anxiety medications. Providing medication to children with autism is only one piece of the puzzle – the reasons for the depression and anxiety must also be addressed.

WEAKNESS IN ORGANIZATIONAL SKILLS AND TASK SEQUENCING

Parents of children with autism frequently report that their child appears to be disorganized both at school and at home. Teachers are often frustrated by the child's inability to keep a clean desk and organize his/her classwork and textbooks. He/she may also have difficulty relaying communications to and from school, keeping track of homework assignments and developing appropriate study skills.

> EXAMPLE I
> The fourth-grade teacher had just given her class an assignment to complete at their desks. Each student was asked to write a brief paragraph about an animal that they liked and why. Mary, a student with autism, appeared to be 'clueless' about how to begin. She began to remove books from her desk as if she was looking for something behind them. Her teacher asked Mary what she was doing and she replied that she didn't know.

> EXAMPLE II
> Joey, a child with autism, was often the last to clean up his desk after his art project. The teacher frequently had to prompt Joey, who would then scramble to finish and get his materials organized.

ACADEMIC AND/OR ATHLETIC SKILL DEFICITS

Sometimes children with autism exhibit poor behaviors because they realize that they lack the academic and athletic skills necessary to complete the task or assignment. They may feel that they are different from their peers in this respect. They may become angry when their deficits are exposed to their classmates and for this reason resent when someone tries to help them.

> EXAMPLE I
> Joey, a 9-year-old boy with Asperger Syndrome, was not very athletic. Although he had some good solid skills associated with running and endurance activities, his upper body strength was weak. In addition, he had trouble with motor planning so that catching and throwing balls were hard for him. When he was in fourth grade, the boys in his physical education class would chide him when he missed the balls. Joey would become very upset when this happened, and would

frequently yell at the other students. For the rest of that school day, his patience would be limited.

The amount of academic trouble that a student is having in core subject areas (reading, math and language arts) will directly impact on his/her ability to continue to be mainstreamed as he/she approaches the upper grades of elementary school. Children with fewer academic needs will have more opportunities to interact with typical children than those who do not. Those children with a need for academic support will eventually be pulled from the classroom for more individualized help. Chapter 4 will provide some general accommodations that can be made for the academically challenged student in the classroom.

DIFFICULTY MANAGING STRESS AND ANXIETY

Parents frequently report that their child with autism can go from a seemingly calm state to one of heightened anxiety in a relatively short period of time. He/she may dwell on negative thoughts, be reduced to tears easily, have explosions of anger and experience difficulty sleeping or eating. Headaches, stomachaches and/or changes in bowel habits become more frequent. It can be heart wrenching to see a child begin to experience these symptoms.

EXAMPLE I

Trisha is a beautiful 13-year-old girl with autism. She has recently moved on to high school as a ninth grader. While other children can easily handle their complex schedule of classes and extracurricular activities, Trisha, by the end of her school day, is exhausted and overwrought. She frequently cannot even attempt to do her homework until well after dinner is over. Her parents would like to see her be more involved in after-school activities but realize that Trisha needs her 'down time.'

Teaching children with autism ways to gauge their anxiety is a necessity in building coping skills. When a child with autism possesses good coping skills, he/she will have a greater chance at continuing in the mainstream and leading a more typical lifestyle.

Many times feelings of anxiety arise when we lose a sense of control over our environment. Feeling powerless or helpless can certainly make us feel anxious. The feelings associated with stress are often those that make us feel our world is spinning out of control. Everyone needs to feel as if he/she has the ability to make decisions and maintain some order in his/her life:

> The design of the brain means that we very often have little or no control over *when* we are swept by emotion, nor over *what* emotion it will be. But we can have some say in *how long* an emotion will last. The issue arises not with garden-variety sadness, worry, or anger; normally such moods pass with time and patience. But when these emotions are of greater intensity and linger past an appropriate point, they shade over into their distressing extremes – chronic anxiety, uncontrollable rage, depression. (Goleman 1995, p.58)

The key to handling anxiety, then, would be to help individuals with autism to manage their anxiety so that it does not linger on or increase in intensity. In Chapter 5, we will provide some strategies to help accomplish this.

ATTENTION PROBLEMS

A common complaint of teachers about children with autism in their classrooms is that they do not pay attention. They appear to be nonfocused or uninterested in the activities at hand. As we have seen previously, this may be due to their language processing abilities, their need for an alternative method of presentation, or their sensory processing problems. Grad Flick (1996, p.2), discusses the various types of attention problems that children may exhibit. He differentiates between *focused attention* (the child's ability to focus on a single topic) and *divided attention* (the child's ability to focus on two or more topics).

> EXAMPLE I
> If Matthew was provided with written directions and then allowed to work on his classwork, he could do so independently. However, if the teacher provided oral directions during the time Matthew was trying to complete the work, he would frequently 'shut down' and not be able to incorporate the new set of instructions.

Flick also discusses *sustained attention* (the ability to focus on tasks to completion) (1996, p.2) and how this could affect a child's performance in the classroom.

> EXAMPLE II
> Jane, a second grader with autism, was finding it difficult to complete worksheets, even if her teacher shortened the number of items she was required to do. Frequently, she had to be prompted time and time again to focus on her paper.

Flick also mentions that *alternating attention* (the ability 'to shift attention between tasks that access different modes of information processing or different response patterns') (1996, p.2) may be a problem for some children.

> EXAMPLE III
> David was having difficulty in many of his high-school classes because of his inability to listen to a lecture, pick out the main idea and then take notes.

Finally, Flick discusses *selective attention*, or the ability to 'tune out' distractions and 'stay tuned' to the main focus (Flick 1996, p.2).

> EXAMPLE IV
> Ryan required a quiet room to complete his classwork. If the door to the classroom was kept open, or if anyone wandered in or out, the work took Ryan double the amount of time it should have taken him to complete it.

Teachers and parents should realize that children with autism may have trouble with some or all of the above. The strategies that are put in place to help with attention problems should match the above problem behaviors that we are trying to support.

At the end of this chapter (Appendix 3.1), the reader can find the continued development of the behavioral support plan for our case study student with autism, Scott, and a possible hypothesis identified for each of his behaviors. Because Scott is actually displaying behaviors for several reasons, three separate pages will be needed for our behavioral support plan.

It should be noted, too, that although the author focused on ten possible causes of misbehavior for children with autism, there could be others. Children may behave poorly when they are ill, because of medication side effects, because they are thirsty or hungry, or because they are not getting enough sleep. These physical hypotheses should also be considered as reasons for poor behavior.

SUMMARY

The purpose of this chapter was to help professionals and parents discover that there are *reasons* why children misbehave:

> Research indicates that prevention [of problem behavior] should be based on the reward of desirable behavior, nonviolent punishment of inappropriate behavior, effective instruction in academic and social skills, and *correction of the environmental conditions that foster deviant behavior.* (Kauffman 1999, p.450)

Because these 'conditions' vary from student to student, *every child's behavior must be examined for its communicative attempt*:

> If we give priority to the least intrusive and least restrictive response to misbehavior rather than to the most effective preventative interventions, then we will forever chase our tail – always and inevitably be ineffectual in preventing the escalation of misbehavior. (Kauffman 1999, p.450)

APPENDIX 3.1

Behavioral Support Plan, page 1

Student name: Scott Smith   **Date:**   February 5, 2002

Define the problem behavior and why it is important to change:

Scott is exhibiting aggression with peers and staff. He is also having crying spells and periods where he yells out.

Hypothesis regarding the problem behavior:

Scott is experiencing some academic skill deficits in reading class and with his fine motor skills in art class.

Identified skill to be taught to reduce problem behavior:

Scott will need to improve his fourth-grade reading skills (especially in comprehension) with the help of his learning support and classroom teacher. He will need additional occupational therapy and practice to develop his fine motor skills in the area of cutting, pasting and handling small items.

Antecedent strategies to put in place to prevent behavior:

Hierarchy of consequential strategies to use when behavior occurs:

Reward system for good behavior:

Methods and dates of data collection for evaluation:

Behavioral Support Plan, page 2

Student name: Scott Smith   **Date:**   February 5, 2002

Define the problem behavior and why it is important to change:

Scott is exhibiting aggression with peers and staff. He is also having crying spells and periods where he yells out.

Hypothesis regarding the problem behavior:

Scott is having problems with transitions.

Identified skill to be taught to reduce problem behavior:

Scott will be able to move through his daily changes in schedule without crying or becoming upset.

Antecedent strategies to put in place to prevent behavior:

Hierarchy of consequential strategies to use when behavior occurs:

Reward system for good behavior:

Methods and dates of data collection for evaluation:

Behavioral Support Plan, page 3

Student name: Scott Smith   **Date:**   February 5, 2002

Define the problem behavior and why it is important to change:

Scott is exhibiting aggression with peers and staff. He is also having crying spells and periods where he yells out.

Hypothesis regarding the problem behavior:

Scott is having sensory integration problems, especially tactile defensiveness.

Identified skill to be taught to reduce problem behavior:

Scott will need to be able to stay calm and not react when he is touched or when people invade his space.

Antecedent strategies to put in place to prevent behavior:

Hierarchy of consequential strategies to use when behavior occurs:

Reward system for good behavior:

Methods and dates of data collection for evaluation:

CHAPTER FOUR

Antecedent Strategies

In James Kauffman's article, 'How We Prevent the Prevention of Emotional and Behavioral Disorders', he discusses problem behaviors:

> Prevention requires identifying specific students in need of more intensive support ... and proactive strategies to address their behavioral needs. If the student is not identified before the problem becomes severe and if the student is not served effectively... the chance for prevention will be lost, as will the chance for the least intrusive and least restrictive intervention. (Kauffman 1999, p.464)

In Chapter 3, we discussed possible hypotheses for poor behavior in children with autism. In this chapter, we will provide some teaching suggestions and strategies to put in place to help prevent the triggers of inappropriate behavior. When the groundwork is put in place in the form of preventative measures that take into consideration the reasons for such behavior (called *antecedent strategies*), tools are provided for the student to enable him/her to avoid the use of these behaviors as a form of communication. This chapter will list, as concisely as possible, antecedent strategies for each of the hypotheses identified in Chapter 3.

LANGUAGE PROCESSING DIFFICULTIES

As we have seen in Chapter 3, problems with receptive language, or the processing of language, may cause students to behave inappropriately as they struggle and become frustrated with their ability to understand what is required of them. Rules and expectations need to be presented concretely, and auditory instruction should be supplemented with visual or tactile techniques to ensure understanding. Teachers can help students with language processing problems in the following ways:

1. Try to eliminate distractions so that the student can concentrate.

2. Speak slowly and clearly. Eliminate extra language and avoid multiple commands. Speak at an appropriate difficulty level for the student.

3. Provide a visual aide to supplement directions, such as a checklist, or a step-by-step list of work to do. Teach the student to check off these items as he/she completes them to maintain his/her attention to the task at hand.

4. To ensure understanding, use visual methods to teach class rules and acceptable ways of behavior and what behaviors will not be tolerated at school.

5. Use a chalkboard or an overhead projector to write important points down as a visual cue for students.

6. Allow time to process a question. Do not re-ask the question unless you have allowed at least ten seconds to pass. Doing so may disrupt the student's thinking process.

7. Use the 'two vocal prompts rule.' If the child does not respond to two vocal prompts at least ten seconds apart, provide a visual prompt or a hand-over-hand prompt on the third try.

8. Ask the child to repeat back to you the directions you have given him/her.

9.   Talk to the student at his/her comprehension level. Remember that some students with autism have excellent expressive language, but this may not be an accurate indicator of their receptive language abilities.

10.   After reading a story, prepare statements that might have been said by the main characters in the story. Have the student read the statement and then have him/her try to write the character's name that could have said it under the statement.

11.   Avoid figures of speech, sarcasm, and idioms. Children with autism are very literal. For example, when speaking about cells in biology, you may need to distinguish this from the cell of a battery. Do not assume that children with autism can make this leap in comprehension. The same applies to phrases like 'under the weather' or 'down in the dumps.' It may be necessary to teach the meaning of idioms by helping the student to use these phrases in sentences and/or recognize the meaning of these phrases in the same.

12.   Do not discourage echolalia. Instead, try to determine the communicative attempt (if any) of the echolalia and respond appropriately. Model for the child more appropriate phrases. Children with autism may use echolalia as a form of communication or to help them process what they hear Because echolalia may be a precursor to more normal speech, it should never be extinguished without consideration of its communicative intent.

EXAMPLE I

One teacher suggests using photos of class members to help teach the class rules. Children were asked to 'act out' the rules while she would take pictures of them. She then prepared a bulletin board displaying each picture with a caption under the picture. For instance, 'No Hitting!' showed a picture of one child pretending to hit another.

EXAMPLE II

Another teacher created a rulebook with one rule on each page. The student was asked to draw a picture above the written words on each page to depict his understanding of the individual rules. When he violated a rule, his teacher would review the book with him.

SOCIAL LANGUAGE DIFFICULTIES

In Moyes (2001) the social inadequacies of children with autism are detailed and suggestions for addressing them are provided. Sadly, these problems are usually not considered as reasons for poor behavior in children with autism, even though we have clearly illustrated in Chapter 3 how such deficits can affect social acceptance. Social skills deficits must always be addressed in individualized education plans, as they are a core symptom of autism spectrum disorders. Educators can help students with these problems in the following ways:

1.   Assume that these children will need to have social language skills taught to them. The best method of doing this is in an individual manner where the skill is introduced, then the skill is practiced in a small group setting (such as a recess group or speech and language class) and then it is prompted and reinforced in a large group setting.

2.   Use drama and role playing to teach voice inflection, modulation and facial expressions.

3.   Use videotape to learn and practice facial expressions and eye contact.

4.   Use trained peers to promote and prompt children in appropriate conversation techniques in naturalistic settings such as lunch time or recess time. This method helps to ensure the use of kid-friendly conversation techniques. If adults do all the teaching, the child's conversations may not sound appropriate to the child's peers.

5. Teach the student conversation openers and how to maintain the topic of conversation by scripting him/her and then practicing it.

EXAMPLE I

One teacher describes her method of teaching the meaning of various idioms to children with autism. The first part of the instruction is one on one, and this is where she introduces the idiom (e.g. 'under the weather' or 'down in the dumps'). The second part provides examples of the proper use of the idiom in word phrases or short stories. Then, in small group instruction, the third part requires students to give back examples of the idiom (e.g. 'When were you fit as a fiddle?') in their own lives. Finally, in large group instruction, a worksheet is provided to determine if the students generalized the material: (e.g. 'Down in the dumps' means which of the following? (a) sad; (b) happy; (c) you work in a garbage dump; (d) you had a fight with your friend.)

EXAMPLE II

One teacher selects brief passages depicting various moods such as happiness, anger, etc. The students then draw on a piece of paper a circle face with the eyes and mouth demonstrating the expression they feel the passage best displays. She introduces this method individually and practices it in small and large group settings.

EXAMPLE III

Another teacher uses a Comic Strip Conversation (Gray 1994a) to teach the child in a one-on-one setting about the importance of turn-taking in conversation. The resulting drawings are saved in a three ring notebook. (Figure 4.1). Later, she prompts him/her in large group settings by referring back to their drawings. References to previous drawings should never be made as a punishment for misbehaviour. Instead, drawings should be reviewed with a positive, proactive attitude and as a joint-social-expedition for teacher and student (of course this approach is equally applicable to good behaviour).

Figure 4.1 The importance of turn-taking in conversation

Source: Adapted from Comic Strips Conversation, Carol Gray, Future Horizons, Arlington, Texas, 1994

EXAMPLE IV

One teacher describes a game that she developed in a social skills camp which she organizes in the summer for children with high-functioning autism. Using a large ball, she demonstrates visually that participating in a conversation is much like tossing a ball back and forth. To keep the conversation going, when you have the ball and it is your turn, you have to be ready with appropriate comments that have to do with the current topic of conversation (Wantuch 2001).

SOCIAL BEHAVIOR DIFFICULTIES

Students with autism also have problems with displaying appropriate social behaviors. Their awkwardness can become evident to peers who may tease or poke fun at them. This will usually prompt inappropriate behavior as they struggle to understand what they are doing wrong. The following may help the students to develop better social behavior skills:

1. Arrange situations for the student where he/she needs to find clues to ascertain how someone is feeling or predict how they will respond. He/she may need to be taught what various facial expressions look like and how various emotions *sound* in one's voice as a precursor to being able to find clues.

2. Use television or videotape to reinforce learning about facial expression(s) and sounds of emotions.

3. Practice scripts and role playing for rehearsing difficult moments such as responding to teasing.

4. Teach the student the rules of several playground games so that he feels confident when joining in. Write social stories to teach appropriate ways to play, win and lose (Figure 4.2).

5. Use visual strategies to teach social behavior.

Social Story for Being A 'Good Sport'

I like to play games.

My favorite games are kickball and baseball.

When we play kickball or baseball, one team will win, and one team will lose.

It will always be this way, unless both teams have the same number of points.

This is called a 'tie' game.

When my team wins a game, I feel very happy. Sometimes I dance, cheer, or yell out:

'Yeah!' My teammates usually feel the same way!

When my team loses, I feel sad. Sometimes I feel angry.

When my team loses, I will not hit, punch, or yell mean things when I am angry.

I will not stomp off the field, throw things, swear, or kick the ground.

When I do these things, people will call me a 'sore loser.'

I will try to be happy for the other team when they win.

I will try to shake the winning team members' hands and congratulate them, just as they congratulate me when my team wins.

They worked hard to win, and they are happy!

There will be other times when my team can win.

Being nice when my team loses is called being a 'good sport.'

When I am a 'good sport,' I will have fun playing games with my friends!

It will not matter who wins or loses.

I know that I did my best.

Figure 4.2 Social Story for being a 'good sport'

EXAMPLE I

Simon Baron-Cohen (2001) developed an instrument whereby students with autism can examine actual pictures of eyes displaying various emotions such as 'friendly,' 'worried,' 'sure about something,' etc. Students are then asked to identify which emotion is being displayed. The instrument measures how well students with autism recognize social communication cues given by the eyes. Teachers can help students to learn this skill by cutting out pictures from magazines and having children learn 'the language of the eyes.'

EXAMPLE II

A student with autism frequently had trouble recognizing that he was invading personal space when speaking to others. He would position his body very close to the listener and cause him/her to be uncomfortable. Vocal reminders that he needed to 'back up' were not effective. His teacher tied a piece of yarn around his waist, leaving a three-foot 'tail.' She instructed the student that most people require three feet of personal space when they are speaking to someone, or they begin to feel uncomfortable. She held out the tail and stretched it in front of him to demonstrate three feet. She had him practice with several of his peers using the tail as a guide. Then she removed the yarn from the student's waist. On the rare occasion when the student forgot the three-foot rule, she handed him a small piece of the yarn, without saying a word, as a prompt. He immediately would retreat to an acceptable distance.

SENSORY PROCESSING DIFFICULTIES

Teachers in regular education classrooms may have little time to make major modifications to the classroom for the sensory processing difficulties of their students. Happily, any modifications that are made prior to the start of the school year are not needed to be made again and will have tremendous influence in helping the child with autism not only to behave appropriately, but also to be more productive in academic work. Teachers can easily implement the following antecedent strategies to address sensory processing difficulties:

1. Refer the student to an occupational therapist for an evaluation that takes into consideration the student's sensory processing difficulties.

2. Discuss with the child's parents his/her sensory issues. Parents often have experienced these problems at home, know their child's reactions, and can forewarn the teacher about sensory difficulties. Discuss with the parent where the child should sit and the modifications that can be made to eliminate sensory processing issues.

3. Plan for ways to address sensory problems such as using a quiet spot or retreat area when a student is overwhelmed. It may be helpful to incorporate the use of this area as a regular part of his/her schedule. This 'escape hatch' can be useful after particularly stimulating times of the day such as gym class, recess, art or music class (Figure 4.3). Teach the student to request the use of his/her escape hatch when he/she is becoming overloaded. This can be done through the use of a social story (Figure 4.4). A distressed student can also present a picture of the quiet spot to his/her teacher when he/she needs to be excused and words are not available.

Figure 4.3 Photo of a quiet spot area (blanket, sit and spin)

4. Make adaptations in the classroom for such differences. For instance, for students who have problems with noise, consider placing felt on the bottom of chair rungs to prevent scraping sounds. Consider preferential seating in the classroom for a student with tactile defensiveness issues. For children with vision disturbances, eliminate busy classroom decorations to free up the number of distractions and allow the student to maintain attention.

Social Story for Using my Quiet Spot

Sometimes, when people touch me, I get really upset.

Sometimes, when there are lots of people around me, I start to feel upset.

I feel like I need to run away.

I feel like I need to yell!

I can tell my teacher or [*insert teacher aide's name here*] I need *to go to my quiet spot to calm down.*

I can say, 'Quiet spot!' when I feel as if I am upset.

I can also show a picture of my quiet spot to my teacher or [*insert teacher aide's name here*] when I feel that I need to go to my quiet spot.

I should try to go to my quiet spot before I shout, cry or hit someone.

I will try to tell my teacher or (*insert teacher aide's name here*) when I need my quiet spot. If I can't, I will show them a picture card of my quiet spot.

They will know what I mean.

I can stay calm in school.

My quiet spot helps me.

Figure 4.4 Social Story for using the quiet spot

5. Use deep pressure activities such as sandwiching the student between beanbags or rolled blankets. It is a common belief that deep pressure activities may help to relieve stress and/or tactile defensiveness.

6. Incorporate periods of repetitive physical activity to help relieve stress (swinging or jogging in the aisle beside student desks). All students will enjoy this as a wake-up activity after a particularly grueling academic lesson. For example, the parents of 7-year-old Mitch knew that swinging was a great stress reliever for him. His individualized education plan (IEP) called for a reserved swing on which Mitch was allowed to swing for the last ten minutes of recess so that he could relieve stress and be more relaxed for afternoon activities.

7. Be aware of the child who shuts down, withdraws, or appears noncommunicative and sleepy as the day progresses. This too may be a sign of sensory processing disorder as he/she attempts to retreat from the things that are disturbing him/her.

8. Avoid the use of perfumes, lotions, or scented deodorants around children with this disability.

9. Do not get into power struggles with a child involving sensory issues. Poor behavior will escalate as he/she struggles to avoid that which distresses him/her.

10. Always approach and touch a child with autism from the front. Try to seat him/her where others will not disturb or bump him/her. Use firm pressure when touching, and make sure that he has anticipated this touch.

11. Provide items for him/her to hold in his/her hand (squeeze toys, textured balls) and manipulate when he/she is becoming stressed. An inexpensive squeeze toy can be made by purchasing a high-quality latex balloon. Use a funnel to fill the balloon with flour, sand, or beans. Knot the balloon when

it is full. The student can squeeze these balloons when he/she is anxious. The different types of textures will help to develop his/her fine motor muscles and sensory processing skills. In addition, it may help to eliminate self-stimulatory movements such as finger flicking or hand flapping.

12. Be aware of fire drills. The student may be able to control his/her reaction and act appropriately during the drill, but for the rest of the day, he/she may be at a heightened anxiety level.

DIFFICULTIES WITH TRANSITIONS AND CHANGE

As we have seen in Chapter 3, many students with autism crave sameness and routine. Students with autism will usually fare best with teachers who are more structured in their daily routines and in their teaching style. Here are some antecedent strategies to help the student with autism who has transition difficulties.

1. Dim the lights when a new activity is about to occur. Couple this with a five-minute verbal warning.

2. Provide the student with a transition warning card that indicates with pictures what is about to come next (Figure 4.5). Prompt the child through a five-minute transition at every minute.

3. Allow the student to move through the transition with his/her teacher assistant or a peer before the other children do.

Figure 4.5 A transition warning card

4. Provide the student, at the beginning of each school day, with a picture schedule of the day's events in the order they will happen. Refer to it often. Do not assume that because your teaching schedule rarely varies that this student does not need a schedule (Figure 4.6).

5. Do not withdraw visual supports because the child 'is doing better.' Just as most of us would not think about throwing away our calendars or planning books, you should refrain from doing so with your student with autism.

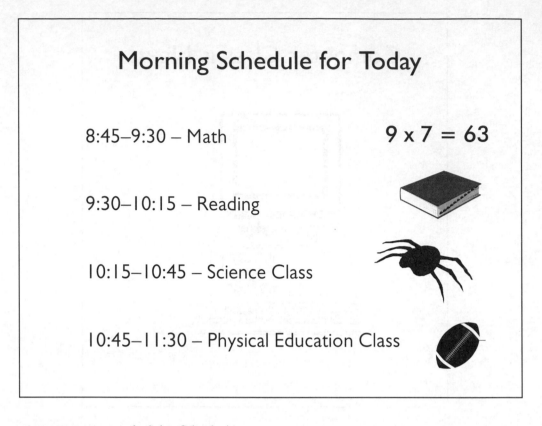

Figure 4.6 Picture schedule of the day's events

PROBLEMS WITH SELF-ESTEEM AND/OR DEPRESSION

Having a positive self-concept is vital to any child's future success. Teachers can help build a student's self-esteem in the following ways:

1. Do not take away rewards previously earned for good behavior because a child demonstrates poor behavior.

2. Reward even minor changes in behavior.

3. Be specific about *behaviors* that are liked and don't use phrases such as 'good boy/or good girl.' (Flick 1996, p.65). Instead say, 'You drew a beautiful tree Larry!' or 'You followed the directions well!' focusing on the particular *behavior* you want to reward.

4. Be sure that there is a difference in the way you handle a student when he is demonstrating incompetence versus noncompliance.

5. Build on the child's strengths (passions). Call attention to what he enjoys doing or can do exceptionally well, despite the unusualness of the activity.

    EXAMPLE I
    Robert, as a child, enjoyed collecting sticks. As he grew older, this hobby developed into him having a vast knowledge of different types of trees and wood. When Robert's parents informed the teacher about this knowledge, his teacher incorporated it into a project that he presented in his science class. Several of the students who did not enjoy team sports at recess began to help Robert find sticks instead.

6. Encourage the student with autism to keep a scrapbook of 'Great Moments': examples of work that he/she is proud of or pictures that mean a lot to him/her. Have him/her review this scrapbook when he/she is feeling 'low.'

7. Make your classroom a safe haven from teasing and bullying. Do not tolerate any occurrences of such.

8. When a child with autism is using negative talk about him/herself, encourage the child to change his/her dialogue. Flick (1996, p.120) states: 'When the parent says, "You didn't put out the garbage", the child who equates this with "I don't help; I'm no good" must learn to change this self-talk to more appropriate comments such as "That's correct, I didn't put out the garbage. I need to do this now." The child can [then] conclude, "I am O.K., my *behavior* needs to change (improve)."'

9. Since many children with autism are visual learners and often dwell on things that have happened to them in the past, teach individual students to replay these scenes like videotape in their heads. After the scene is replayed, have the students describe a new, happier ending to the video.

10. 'Remember that it takes at least five, and perhaps up to ten, positive comments to counteract one negative one.' (Flick 1996, pp.122–3).

11. Make sure that teacher aides and therapeutic staff support personnel are not merely following the student around prompting him/her all day, or worse yet completing the work for him/her. (The author refers to these individuals as 'Velcro aides' because of their willingness to stick to the child wherever he/she goes.) They should be providing the student with as much independence as possible. This can be accomplished by creating visual supports (checklists, written sets of directions, modified work, etc.) so that the child can experience success *on his/her own*.

12. Be sure that you respect the child's privacy and maintain confidentiality with regards to his/her grades, accommodations, health concerns, etc.

WEAKNESS IN ORGANIZATION SKILLS AND TASK SEQUENCING

There are many strategies teachers can put into place to help the student with autism improve his organizational/study skills:

1. Use a homework assignment book or sheet (Figure 4.7). Have the teacher initial it at the end of the day. Reward the child for accuracy. When the child has finished his/her homework, parents should also initial it and reward accuracy.

2. After the child's book bag has been packed to go home, have the teacher double-check it.

3. Provide a quiet spot, free from distractions, to complete homework. Homework and studying should always be done in this spot. A child's bed is not an appropriate place to do homework, as this is also the place he/she sleeps or relaxes; the same for the place where he/she watches television.

Homework Assignments

Today's date _____

Math	Social Studies	Science	Health	Spelling

Teacher agrees this is accurate and student has brought home all the necessary books.

_____

Parent agrees that homework was done and student has brought assignments and books back to school.

_____

Figure 4.7 Homework assignment sheet

4.   Set aside a certain time of the day for homework completion. Scheduled homework times should be structured but flexible, according to the child's needs. For instance, if the student needs to unwind at the end of the day or is involved in a social activity, he/she may benefit from having homework time after supper. For others, especially those who procrastinate, completing homework right after school or after a brief snack may be useful. Even if there are no homework assignments, it may be beneficial to have some educational activity (such as reading a book or writing a letter) completed during this block of time so that the child is conditioned to this period as being set aside for academic work.

MORNING BOOKS	*AFTERNOON BOOKS*
Reading	Science
Math	Social Studies
Spelling	Health
Pencils and erasers	

The left side of my desk should have the above books in the order of the map. The right side of my desk should also have the above books in the correct order. My pencils and erasers should be in the slot in front of my books.

Figure 4.8 Desk map

5.   Use a desk map to help keep the child's desk neat (Figure 4.8). The map can be laminated and placed on top of the child's desk.

6.   For older students, use color-coded notebooks, and folders or binders for morning subjects and afternoon subjects.

7.   Provide the student with a 'housekeeping day' to help eliminate unnecessary papers in his/her desk, locker, or folders.

8.   Students with autism may not be able to look at a task and discern the sequence of steps that the project needs to be completed. To help the student get organized, have him/her write down any thoughts he/she may have about how the project could be completed. Then, have him/her order those steps. You may need to supply missing information. He/she can then use these steps as an organizational tool for completing the task. An outline of work can also be created by using fill-in-the-blank questions. For instance: 'What am I to do for this assignment?' 'When is this assignment due?' 'Do I need to obtain any outside materials to help me complete this assignment?'

9.   Modify assignments. Often it takes this student a longer period of time to accomplish work that other children can do in several minutes. For this reason, he/she should have shorter assignments.

10. Prioritize assignments. If it is too stressful to finish all homework, the most important homework could be done first.

11. Do not require the student with handwriting difficulties to use this skill for everything. Encourage the use of a wordprocessor, typewriter, or even a tape recorder. The use of such items should be listed in the student's individualized education plan (IEP) as an assistive technology device.

12.   Modify and reduce homework assignments. For instance, using a highlighter, mark off only the problems you feel are necessary on a homework sheet for the child to show mastery of the task at hand. Make sure assignments are not busy work.

13.   Provide more time on assessments and adapt assessments in length, or provide two or three choices for each multiple-choice type question, instead of four or five. Use a 'word bank': the student can choose the correct answer from a group of words provided as possible answers.

14.   Provide written directions to assessments and assignments.

15.   Consider the use of an extra set of textbooks for home use.

16.   Use a calendar to mark the day when long-term assignments/projects are due and then also mark the date when the student must begin work on this project.

17.   Assign a 'homework buddy', another student who can be called after school when the student with autism has questions about an assignment.

18.   Consider the use of a peer note-taker. This peer's notes can be compared after class to make sure the student with autism has no gaps in his/her notes.

19.   Give the student modified outlines for class note-taking and homework. He/she can then fill in the blanks and use these sheets as study guides.

20.   Consider the use of a student mailbox system for communication of papers, assignments, etc.

EXAMPLE I

One teacher used empty 28 oz cans with the tops and bottoms removed and placed them on a rack. Each can had a student's name on it. She would place all papers going to the student in his/her can.

ACADEMIC SKILL DEFICITS

As explained in Chapter 3, there are many times when the student with autism may experience skill deficits in one or more subject areas in the general education classroom. There exists a fine line where on the one side a child is receiving educational benefit in this subject area from his/her placement in the general education classroom and on the other side the child could have greater academic benefit if he/she were pulled out for one-on-one instruction. Regular education teachers can and should make modifications to their teaching for students exhibiting academic difficulty, but it may not be enough. When consideration is being given to changing a child's placement from the least restrictive setting (general education classroom) to a more specialized setting, teachers can ask themselves the following questions to ensure that the team is making the right decision:

1.   Have I provided visual and/or tactile methods of teaching this subject, or do I primarily rely on oral presentation techniques? Consider that some students learn best when alternative approaches are used.

EXAMPLE 1
A business education teacher frequently instructed students on how to write personal checks in a lecture-style presentation. One year, she made a large-scale copy of a personal check and had it laminated. She taped this visual aide to the chalkboard and obtained a grease magic marker. She had each of the students approach the board and complete the check with the information she provided orally. In this way, the students had hands-on practice writing the check and could learn from each other.

2.   Have I modified classwork and homework assignments for this student?

3.   Have I utilized a teacher aide or peer support or provided extra help for this student in my classroom?

4.   Have I had a brainstorming session with the child's parents on ways to help him/her improve his/her performance? Do I regularly communicate with the parents regarding the student's difficulties and successes?

5.   Have I enlisted all school supports that are available to this student (reading lab, instructional support, tutoring)?

6.   Have I looked into having the school purchase supplemental materials for this student (computer software packages, manipulatives) or asked my building principal if these items are available? (It should be noted that many children with autism have a medical assistance card because of their disability and that this card can be used to purchase such items at no cost to the school district.)

7.   Have I established some one-on-one time with myself and the student?

8.   Have I created a motivation or reward system for the student to encourage him/her when he/she succeeds?

9.   Have I ensured that the materials (textbook, worksheets, tests) are all at the student's instructional level?

10.   Have I modified the grading system (allowed test retakes, added extra credit items, etc.) so that this particular child can experience some success?

If all of the above have been tried and the child still struggles with poor grades and an escalating number of inappropriate behaviors, the entire team will know that it is time to consider a new placement.

DIFFICULTY MANAGING STRESS AND ANXIETY

Helping children with autism to manage anxiety and stress is extremely important to preventing inappropriate behavior:

> Children with sensory processing difficulties [as in children with autism] ... are especially prone to extreme anxiety because it's more difficult for them to regulate, comprehend, and operate on their social and physical worlds. It is, therefore, particularly easy for children with special needs to become involved in these cycles of anxiety and fragmented thinking. (Baron-Cohen 2001 pp.26-7)

The following antecedent strategies can easily be incorporated into the student's day:

1. Maintain a firm schedule for bedtime, even on weekends and vacations. Fluctuating schedules can cause the child to be too tired and emotionally 'raw.'

2. Use imagery to refocus anxious thoughts. For instance, when the child is experiencing a thought that frightens or stresses him/her, have him/her scribble it out in his/her imagination and replace it with a relaxing picture.

3. Teach the child deep breathing exercises. When the student is becoming anxious or stressed, remove him/her from the location and take him/her to a quiet area where he/she can practice these exercises. Help the student to become aware of his/her heart rate and learn to slow it down when he/her is anxious.

4. Build into the child's schedule time for vigorous exercise. Exercise can do much to reduce the child's stress level.

5. Teach the child 'self-talk' methods: for instance, having him/her say, 'I can do this ... I don't need to yell ... I will

just try my best and see what happens.' Providing a prompt card with the same may be useful.

6.   Invest in a relaxation tape that can be used with headphones in a quiet spot.

7.   As mentioned previously in this chapter, create a quiet spot complete with headphones, soft music, and pillows that the student can access when he/she needs to.

8.   Be sure to allow time for relaxation in the child's day. Too often, children with autism have full school days, planned social activities, and therapeutic appointments after school, allowing little time to relax once homework is completed.

9.   Help the child to identify his stress level and communicate this to his teacher and parents. Dr Tony Attwood shares with us that visual methods are helpful such as the 'stress barometer' (Figure 4.9). The 'stress barometer' can also depict what the student needs to do once he has identified that his stress has reached a certain level:

10.   As we have stated before, some children with autism have passions that help them to relax, such as using computers, playing with or reading about trains or watching favorite videos. Teachers can incorporate some of these into specific parts of the school day to enable a child with anxiety issues to unwind.

ATTENTION PROBLEMS

Attention problems can lead to poor behavior. It is often assumed that a child is noncompliant when he doesn't pay attention to directions or is not focused and on task. The following are ways that teachers can assist a child with autism to address attentiveness:

My Stress Barometer

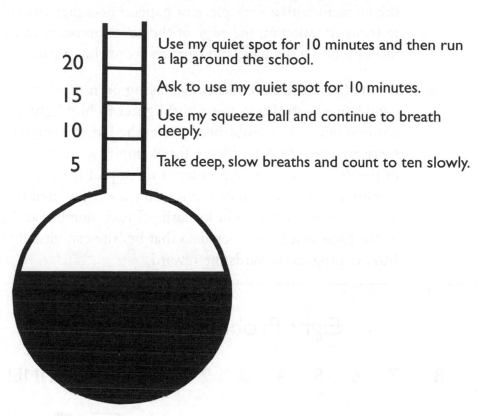

20   Use my quiet spot for 10 minutes and then run a lap around the school.

15   Ask to use my quiet spot for 10 minutes.

10   Use my squeeze ball and continue to breath deeply.

5   Take deep, slow breaths and count to ten slowly.

Figure 4.9 Stress barometer

1. Eliminate distractions from the student's desk. The student should have as few items as possible on the top of the desk at any one time. It has been suggested that dark-colored desktops are more conducive to maintaining attention than light-colored ones. If dark-colored desktops are not available, one can be made by taping black construction paper to the top of the desk.

2. Purchase a tilt board so that material can be raised up and placed closer to eye level as opposed to being flat on the desk.

3. When completing a worksheet or reading a book, have the student cover up text or problems that are not being used at the moment with a dark piece of paper. Encourage the child to focus attention on the edge of the cover-up paper as he/she moves it down the page and exposes words line by line.

4. For students who have difficulty staying on task when completing worksheets, use a highlighter to highlight a reduced number of problems that he/she has to complete. If there are seven such problems, for example, write the number of problems in descending order at the top of the page and a reward that he/she will earn once they are completed (Figure 4.10). Encourage the child to slash off each number at the top of the page as it is completed so that he/she can visually see his/her progress towards the reward.

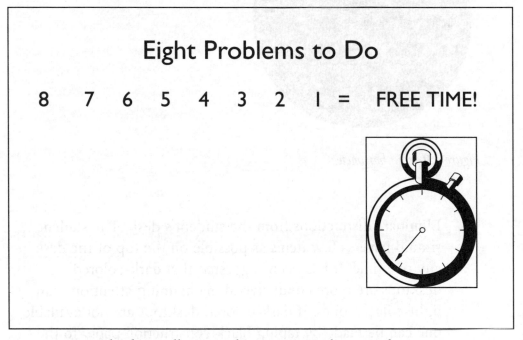

Figure 4.10 Number line to illustrate task progress towards a reward

5. Teach the student how one's body should look when paying attention. Dr Grad Flick states that modeling the behavior you wish to establish can be most effective:

A parent can demonstrate the notion of 'paying attention' versus getting 'off task' to the child. For example, a story might be recorded on tape so that the total story time can be determined; the parent could then demonstrate attending by first listening and then periodically engaging in other behavior, e.g., playing with a pencil, looking around the room, etc. It will be the child's task to judge when the parent is attending or not attending. The child may then reverse roles and it will be the parent's turn to see how much the child is on or off task. This type of exercise with parent and child would be more beneficial in promoting greater *awareness* of when the child is attending (on task) and not attending (off task) rather than having the effect of expanding attentional processes directly ... Simply telling a child to pay attention or stay on task does not appear to be effective. If it were, parents and teachers would not need to say that as often as they do. (Flick 1996, pp.42–4)

6. Flick (1996) also recommends the use of a nonverbal clue (such as tugging on one's earlobe) and explaining this choice to the student so that the teacher can provide this cue to him/her when he/she is not paying attention. This will eliminate the embarrassment of calling out his/her name.

7. A good measure of attention may be drawn from the student's ability to recall information from what was presented when he/she did not appear to be paying attention. It is important to understand that some children cannot visually attend to a teacher but are still able to maintain attention in their work. If they are told to attend visually, they may lose the ability to comprehend as they may have difficulty doing the two processes at once.

8. Before difficult activities, provide students with the reward procedure *before beginning the work*. For instance, a chart is presented before beginning the task that depicts how many problems need to be completed, how many of those problems need to be correct or how much of a story needs to be read

before earning a high-interest reward. Often times, high-interest rewards consist of those items that captivate these children the most.

EXAMPLE I

Richard loved electronics. His teacher discovered that using this interest was a tremendous motivator for him to complete his classwork. Richard had a reward chart where he could earn tokens that could be used towards free time to look through electronic magazines if he completed his math problems.

9. Alternate between high and low interest activities. Separate low interest activities with breaks.

10. Arrange for tests and difficult assignments to be completed in quiet rooms away from distractions.

11. Choose projects with short-term attainable goals.

12. Use study corrals when the student is completing important work such as tests or graded assignments so he/she won't be distracted by fellow classmates.

13. Cut and fold worksheets into fourths, sixths, eighths, etc., so that a minimum number of problems are in the child's line of vision at any one time.

14. Use graph paper for math problems to eliminate careless mistakes in lining up decimals and digits.

15. Use materials that have quick feedback or are self-rewarding.

16. Seat the child near students who are good models.

17. Vary the method of teacher presentation. Move around the room while teaching. Use the chalkboard or overhead projector. If the presentation is primarily auditory, incorporate visual or tactile components to help reach students who learn in different ways.

EXAMPLE I

Students in Mrs Phillips's class were learning to alphabetize. To add more meaning to the lesson, she designed a hands-on laminated manila folder with pictures of student desks. Glued to each desk was a tiny magnet. Included with the folder was a 'pocket' containing student's names, each one typed on a separate miniature card. On the back of each typed card was a tiny magnet. The students were required to place the name cards on the desks so that the desks were arranged in alphabetical order. The magnets held the cards firmly to the desks. When the students completed this task, they could self-check their work by turning the folder over and opening a small 'door' (also held shut with magnets) to reveal the correct alphabetical placement of the desks.

The antecedent strategies provided in this chapter can be easily incorporated into the general education classroom by teachers and parents who are truly motivated to solve the behavior problems that make inclusion of children with autism in those typical classrooms difficult. Indeed, if such antecedent strategies are not adopted, then the supports that the child with autism desperately needs will be lacking and the problem behaviors will continue. The child with autism should not be found at fault for having a disability that makes it difficult for him to behave as typical children do. Antecedent strategies, when appropriately designed and consistently applied, are the building blocks used to shape and define the course of student behavior.

At the conclusion of this chapter can be found the continuation of the behavioral support plan for Scott Smith, our case study student with autism (Appendix 4.1). Various antecedent strategies from this chapter were chosen as appropriate for helping to address Scott's behaviors.

APPENDIX 4.1

Behavioral Support Plan, page 1

Student name: Scott Smith   **Date:**   February 5, 2002

Define the problem behavior and why it is important to change:

Scott is exhibiting aggression with peers and staff. He is also having crying spells and periods where he yells out.

Hypothesis regarding the problem behavior:

Scott is experiencing some academic skill deficits in reading class and deficits in his fine motor skills in art class.

Identified skill to be taught to reduce problem behavior:

Scott will need to improve his fourth-grade reading skills (especially in comprehension) with the help of his learning support and classroom teacher. He will need additional occupational therapy and practice to develop his fine motor skills in the area of cutting, pasting and handling small items.

Antecedent strategies to put in place to prevent behavior:

- Scott will attend learning support for reading each day for the second half of reading.
- Scott will place his pencil horizontally on his desk to cue his teacher when he needs help.
- Scott will be provided with modified worksheets and tests, and directions will be written in the form of a checklist for Scott. His parents will be given blank story maps to use at home.
- Scott will receive additional occupational therapy, and his parents will be given exercises to use with Scott at home.
- Scott will be given a social story about aggression and this will be reviewed with Scott so that he can know what his consequences will be when he is aggressive [*See Figure 6.1 in Chapter 6*].
- Scott will be provided with a social story to explain his reward system [*see Figure 5.11* in Chapter 5].

Hierarchy of consequential strategies to use when behavior occurs:

Reward system for good behavior:

Methods and dates data collection for evaluation:

Behavioral Support Plan, page 2

Student name: Scott Smith   **Date:** February 5, 2002

Define the problem behavior and why it is important to change:

Scott is exhibiting aggression with peers and staff. He is also having crying spells and periods where he yells out.

Hypothesis regarding the problem behavior:

Scott is having problems with transitions.

Identified skill to be taught to reduce problem behavior:

Scott will move through the daily changes in his school schedule without crying or becoming upset.

Antecedent strategies to put in place to prevent behavior:

- Scott will be provided each day with a picture schedule of his daily schedule. His teacher assistant will review it with him each day. He will also have changes alerted to him as soon as they become available.

- Scott will be given five-minute warnings before transitions are about to take place by his teacher or teacher's aide, and his picture schedule will be reviewed with him.

- If Scott seems to be having a particularly stressful day, his teacher assistant will move Scott through his transition before the other children (i.e. take him to his other classes one minute earlier).

- Scott's social stories [*see p.1* of *this plan*] will be used to introduce his rewards and consequences.

Hierarchy of consequential strategies to use when behavior occurs:

Reward system for good behavior:

Methods and dates of data collection for evaluation:

Behavioral Support Plan, page 3

Student name: Scott Smith   **Date:**   Feburary 5, 2002

Define the problem behavior and why it is important to change:

Scott is exhibiting aggression with peers and staff. He is also having crying spells and periods where he yells out.

Hypothesis regarding the problem behavior:

Scott is having sensory integration problems, especially tactile defensiveness.

Identified skill to be taught to reduce problem behavior:

Scott will be able to stay calm and not overreact when he is touched or when people invade his space.

Antecedent strategies to put in place to prevent behavior:

- Scott's occupational therapist will focus on some activities to help with tactile sensory processing.
- Scott will be provided with a quiet spot and a social story to teach him about the use of his quiet spot [see Figure 4.4, Chapter 4]. He will also be provided with a picture card of the quiet spot.
- Scott's teacher's aide will review the stress barometer with Scott when he appears to be stressed, and guide him through the relaxation strategies associated with it [see Figure 4.9, Chapter 4].
- Scott's assistant will provide him with a stress ball to squeeze during stressful times of the day.
- Scott will be assigned the last place in moving and waiting lines to avoid excess tactile stimulation.
- Scott's desk will be placed on the end of a table arrangement in the classroom for the same reason as above.
  Scott's social stories [see p.1 of this plan] will be used to introduce his rewards and consequences.

Hierarchy of consequential strategies to use when behavior occurs:

Reward system for good behavior:

Methods and dates of data collection for evaluation:

CHAPTER 5

Rewards and Motivators

An important part of any behavioral support plan is the reinforcement tools that we put in place to encourage appropriate classroom behavior. Their importance to the success of the plan cannot be overemphasized. Punishment teaches children with autism that they have done something wrong, but it doesn't teach these children what behaviors are acceptable. Reinforcing or rewarding positive behavior does. Teachers and parents need to realize that motivators for a particular student can change. It is important to continually identify what types of rewards are most effective for each student. Rewards can include edible reinforcers (candy, gum, fruit), material reinforcers (stickers, stamps, toys, puzzles), social reinforcers (smiling, patting, nodding, shaking hands) or activity-type reinforcers (having free time, sprinkling glitter, watching a movie). There exists a vast array of choices in each of the above categories that can help to teach students with autism the appropriate behavior in both social and academic situations. We only need to discover them to unlock their power.

DISCOVERING EFFECTIVE REWARD SYSTEMS

The most effective reward system for any child is one that is meaningful to that particular child. One way to ensure that rewards are meaningful is to discover what special interests or 'passions' the student has from his parents. William Stillman (a self-diagnosed adult with Asperger Syndrome) describes his passion for the *Wizard of Oz* (Moyes 2001, p.128) and how he would have been more motivated to learn math skills as a child if this interest had been incorporated into his lessons by his teacher. Creative teachers can use these passions to develop lesson plans that will not only encourage student participation, but will also enable him/her to 'shine' as an expert in his/her area of interest. Consider the following examples of some talented students with autism.

Figure 5.1 Steven

Steven (Figure 5.1), as a first-grade student, was exceptional at decoding reading words. His teacher would frequently arrange for him to peer tutor other children who were not so gifted in this area.

Figure 5.2 Matthew

Matthew (Figure 5.2) had a passion for studying weather patterns. Each day, his teacher would allow Matthew to present the 'minute for weather.' He would describe daily barometric and temperature readings and give a weather forecast to the class. This also served as a transition device between home and school as it occurred first thing in the morning. It enabled him to go to school without resistance as he looked forward to his presentation.

Figure 5.3 Brett

Brett (Figure 5.3) has a real interest and talent in working with electronics and electrical devices. As a young child he created an alarm system for his room so that the alarm would go off if his sibling entered. His teacher incorporated a reward system to use this interest in helping him to complete his classwork. If Brett completed his work, he was able to design and create electronic devices during school and demonstrate them for his class.

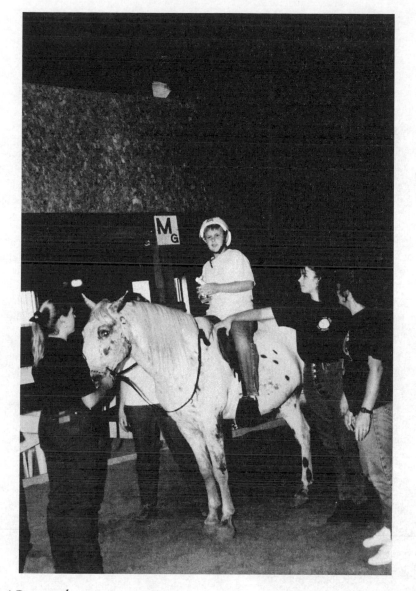

Figure 5.4 Raymond

Raymond (Figure 5.4) had a particular interest in country western music. His teacher allowed Raymond to listen to country western music (in particular the group Alabama) when he successfully completed his classwork. This type of music was also used as a form of relaxation when he became stressed.

Figure 5.5 Rosemarie

Rosemarie (Figure 5.5) had a gift in drawing. Today, she designs cards for publication. Because Rosemarie had limited communication as a youngster, her teachers would often have Rosemarie draw pictures to communicate. She also had a fondness for horses, as seen in many of her drawings (Figure 5.6).

Figure 5.6 Rosmarie's drawing of a horse

Discovering what rewards are most meaningful to a student can also be accomplished by having the student complete a small discovery worksheet such as the one found in Figure 5.7. The student can then communicate to the teacher potential motivators. This tool will serve as a good reference point to design a behavioral support plan that will be tailored to the student's particular needs.

What Motivates You?

Directions: Read each item in the left column. Put a check mark under (1) if it is not very important to you, (2) if it is somewhat important to you or (3) if it is very important to you.

	1	2	3
Having a snack in class			
Having free time in class			
Going to the library			
Earning extra credit points			
Having no homework			
Doing puzzles or games in class			
Having teachers write notes when I am good			
Reading my favorite book or magazine in class			
Listening to music in class			
Earning stickers			
Using the internet in class			
Playing computer games in class			
Studying or having class outside			
Describe your interests and things you like to do:			

Figure 5.7 Discovery worksheet

If a particular student identifies that having no homework is a strong motivator for him/her, a homework pass can be designed and distributed when he/she completes his/her classwork with no problem behaviors (Figure 5.8). 'Free time' cards can also be used for granting students with autism 'a break' from work after they have performed well and maintained attention to task (Figure 5.9).

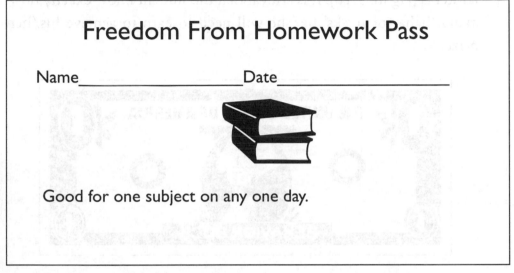

Figure 5.8 Freedom from homework pass

Figure 5.9 Free time card

For rewards that are more tangible, it is often helpful for students to earn the purchase of such rewards in increments. The rewards that the student designates as most important to him/her on his/her worksheet can be assigned a dollar amount. When the student maintains positive behaviors over a predetermined period of time, he/she may earn a 'behavior buck' that can be used to purchase those particular items (Figure 5.10). It is critical that the student know exactly how many 'behavior bucks' he/she will need to earn to achieve his/her prize.

Figure 5.10 Reward of a 'behavior buck'

It is prudent to reward the student frequently when he/she demonstrates positive behavior so that he/she can immediately see the benefit of practicing appropriate behavior.

ADDITIONAL IDEAS FOR REWARD SYSTEMS

Token system

When the student completes a task, a token is awarded and placed in a clear jar marked with his/her name. When the jar is full or reaches a certain designated level, the child earns a reward. Marbles or plastic poker chips can serve as tokens. Tokens should not be removed for inappropriate behavior. Also, the student will need to know what desired behavior is required to earn a token before the system begins. Social stories are easy ways to explain reward systems to children with autism (Figure 5.11).

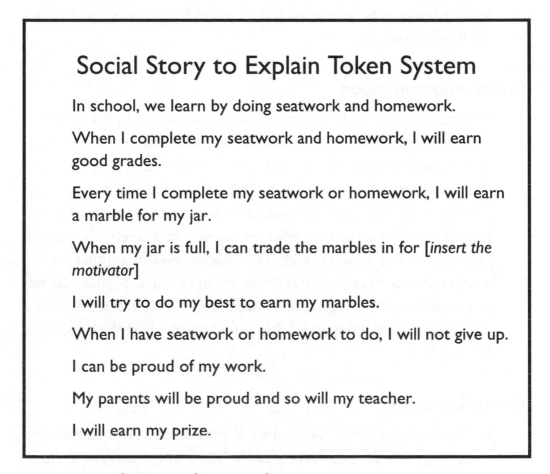

Social Story to Explain Token System

In school, we learn by doing seatwork and homework.

When I complete my seatwork and homework, I will earn good grades.

Every time I complete my seatwork or homework, I will earn a marble for my jar.

When my jar is full, I can trade the marbles in for [*insert the motivator*]

I will try to do my best to earn my marbles.

When I have seatwork or homework to do, I will not give up.

I can be proud of my work.

My parents will be proud and so will my teacher.

I will earn my prize.

Figure 5.11 Social story to explain a reward system

Points earned vs. points lost program

This program works well for the student whose behavior is all over the place on one particular day. It also serves as a consequence program. To begin, the student is presented with a list of acceptable behaviors and the point value assigned to each. A list of unacceptable behaviors is presented in the same way. As the student moves through the day, he/she earns points, but poor behavior subtracts points from the accumulated total. The number of points he/she has remaining at the end

of the day earn certain rewards (also based on point values and designated by a list to the student). Points do not carry over to the next day.
This plan can be designed to anticipate exactly what behaviors the
teacher is trying to extinguish and to assign a point value to each according to severity.

Communication report

Communicating with parents about a student's behavior often
promotes home/school cooperation and provides another way to posi-
tively reinforce how the student behaved in school (Figure 5.12).
When parents are notified of a child's positive behavior, this serves as
another opportunity for the student to be rewarded for good work.
Parents can then set up their own reward system whereby the amount
of good work at school can be accumulated towards another reward
which the student can enjoy at home. As an example, a child who has
an interest in computer games may need to earn 60 points from his/her
teacher's report in order for his/her parents to purchase the latest game
for him/her.

The sticker card

In this reward system, the student is presented with a sticker card
consisting of a 20-grid rectangle. He/she earns a sticker (or check
mark) on his/her card in one square when he/she demonstrates good
behavior. When his/her card is filled, he/she can trade the card in for a
reward. He/she then begins a new card. Choosing stickers that match
the student's interests can be most effective.

Positive notes

A positive or encouraging word can mean everything to the student.
When put in writing, it can be another great way for parents to
continue to reward the student for excellent behavior. Since many

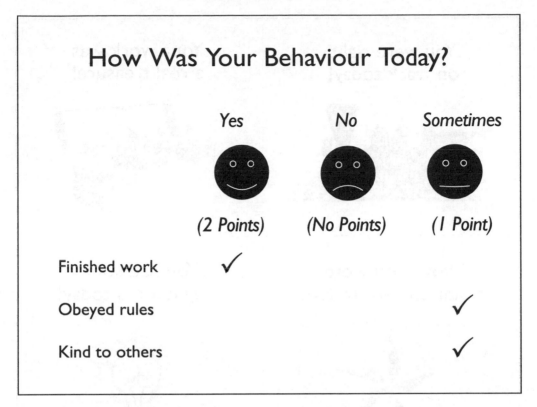

Figure 5.12 A communication report

students with autism are visual learners, pictures can be incorporated as well into the notes (Figure 5.13).

Students who frequently exhibit poor behavior often do not hear many positive words about themselves from their peers or the adults close to them. Often, as teachers, we must make a conscious effort not only to see the positive in our students, but also to share it with them. Children who are frequently reprimanded for poor behavior will come to see themselves as 'bad,' and this will often lead to a display of even more problem behaviors. The number of positive words that are said to a student can be compared to a self-esteem savings account. The student deposits into his/her 'account' all the positive words that have been said to him/her. When he/she must be reprimanded for his/her behavior, he/she will be able to withdraw from the account the positive words as he/she needs them and be less likely to internalize or

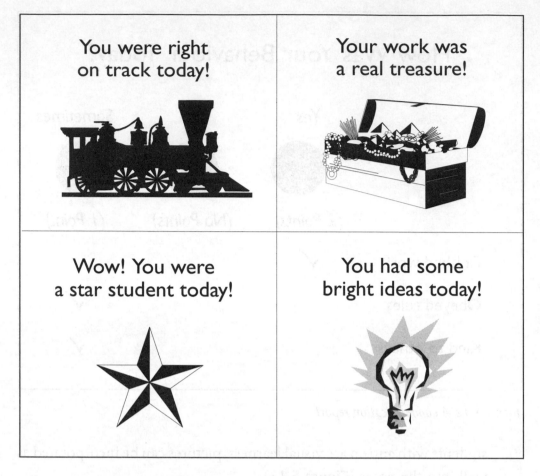

Figure 5.13 Positive notes of encouragement for the students

'deposit' the negative ones. Comments such as 'Hey Joey, nice try!' or 'Kathy that was really good thinking!' or 'Bill, you stuck to it, didn't you?' can offer tremendous amounts of encouragement to students. Teachers need to be careful that compliments are sincere, and again are based on the student's *behavior*, not the student him/herself.

Cancel cards

When a student does a good job, a 'cancel card' can be used to cancel out a consequence that he/she may have been given earlier in the day. This serves as a chance for the student to redeem him/herself and to reinforce (reward) his/her effort for complying at later times during the day (Figure 5.14). Some teachers also use the cancel cards as a reward to be earned. Students can then present these cards when they are about to receive a consequence. Teachers will need to explain to the student ahead of time which kinds of consequences the cancel cards can be used for and for what types of behaviors they won't be accepted. It is sad to see a student serving out a consequence for problem behavior that occurred much earlier and has not surfaced again. Cancel cards work well in acknowledging to a student that he/she has made up for his/her previous poor behavior and his/her consequence has been forgiven.

Figure 5.14 Cancel card to acknowledge effort

Contract system

For older students, it may be difficult to encourage successful completion of work and class participation in subjects which may be difficult or not have meaning for them. It may be useful to develop a contract system whereby the students agree to do a certain number of assignments to receive the grade of their choice. For instance, in

English Literature class, Figure 5.15 shows the requirements one teacher contracted with a student for him to be able to earn an A grade. Notice that the student will sign his name to the contract and he will receive the letter grade with the amount of work that he has agreed to do.

SUMMARY

To summarize, there are six basic guidelines when implementing a reward/motivation system for students with autism:

1. Choose rewards that are meaningful to the student.

2. In the beginning, reward the student often and as he/she comes close to appropriate behavior. Later, you can be more selective as to what behaviors you will reward.

3. Make sure that the student understands the reward system and what behavior earns the reward.

4. Incorporate 'passions' into lesson plans to encourage motivation.

5. For consistency, involve the parents in creation of the reward plan and to allow the student extra opportunities to earn rewards for positive behavior.

6. Do not take away rewards that have previously been earned.

English Literature Grading Contract

Name _____ Date _____

To earn an A grade, the following are required:

1. Write a five-page or more double-spaced typed short story on a subject of you choice.

2. Read three short stories or six poems by authors from the author's list and write two paragraphs with at least five sentences each as follows:

    (a) first paragraph: what the poem/story was about, including the name of the author and the title of the work.

    (b) second paragraph: your impressions and opinions.

3. Watch two films from the classics film list and summarize each in a double-spaced, one-page typed report. The report should describe what the film was about and your impressions.

4. All work (no exceptions) is due by _____.

I agree to perform the above work to earn an A grade for this class.

_____ (Signature of student)

Figure 5.15 Contract system

APPENDIX 5.1

Behavioral Support Plan, page 1

Student name: Scott Smith   **Date:**   February 5, 2001

Define the problem behavior and why it is important to change:

Scott is exhibiting aggression with peers and staff. He is also having crying spells and periods where he yells out.

Hypothesis regarding the problem behavior:

Scott is experiencing some academic skill deficits in reading class and deficits in his fine motor skills in art class.

Identified skill to be taught to reduce problem behavior:

Scott will need to improve his fourth-grade reading skills (especially in comprehension) with the help of his learning support and classroom teacher. He will need additional occupational therapy and practice to develop his fine motor skills in the area of cutting, pasting and handling small items.

Antecedent strategies to put in place to prevent behavior:

- Scott will attend learning support for reading each day for the second half of reading.
- Scott will place his pencil horizontally on his desk to cue his teacher when he needs help.
- Scott will be provided with modified worksheets and tests, and directions will be written in the form of a checklist for Scott. His parents will be given blank story maps to use at home.
- Scott will receive additional occupational therapy, and his parents will be given exercises to use with Scott at home.
- Scott will be given a social story about aggression and this will be reviewed with Scott so that he can know what his consequences will be when he is aggressive [see Figure 6.1, in Chapter 6].
- Scott will be provided with a social story to explain his reward system [see Figure 5.11 in Chapter 5).

Hierarchy of consequential strategies to use when behavior occurs:

Reward system for good behavior:

- ○ Token system to earn airplane-related rewards: magazines, models, etc. [*see Figure 5.11, Chapter 5*].
- ○ Positive notes to student [see *Figure 5.13, Chapter 5*].
- ○ Notes to parents [see *Figure 5.12, Chapter 5*].

Methods and dates of data collection for evaluation:

Behavioral Support Plan, page 2

Student name: Scott Smith   **Date:**   February 5, 2001

Define the problem behavior and why it is important to change:

Scott is exhibiting aggression with peers and staff. He is also having crying spells and periods where he yells out.

Hypothesis regarding the problem behavior:

Scott is having problems with transitions.

Identified skill to be taught to reduce problem behavior:

Scott will move through the daily changes in his school schedule without crying or becoming upset.

Antecedent strategies to put in place to prevent behavior:

- ° Scott will be provided each day with a picture schedule of his daily schedule. His teacher assistant will review it with him each day. He will also have changes alerted to him as soon as they become available.

- ° Scott will be given five-minute warnings before transitions are about to take place by his teacher or teacher's aide, and his picture schedule will be reviewed with him.

- ° If Scott seems to be having a particularly stressful day, his teacher assistant will move Scott through his transition before the other children (i.e. take him to his other classes one minute earlier).

- ° Scott's social stories [*see p.1 of this plan*] will be used to introduce his rewards and consequences.

Hierarchy of consequential strategies to use when behavior occurs:

Reward system for good behavior:

- ○ Token system to earn airplane-related rewards: magazines, models, etc. [*see Figure 5.11, Chapter 5*].
- ○ Positive notes to student [*see Figure 5.13, Chapter 5*].
- ○ Notes to parents [*see Figure 5.12*, Chapter 5].

Methods and dates of data collection for evaluation:

Behavioral Support Plan, page 3

Student name: Scott Smith   **Date:** February 5, 2001

Define the problem behavior and why it is important to change:

Scott is exhibiting aggression with peers and staff. He is also having crying spells and periods where he yells out.

Hypothesis regarding the problem behavior:

Scott is having sensory integration problems, especially tactile defensiveness.

Identified skill to be taught to reduce problem behavior:

Scott will be able to stay calm and not overreact when he is touched or when people invade his space.

Antecedent strategies to put in place to prevent behavior:

- ○ Scott's occupational therapist will focus on some activities to help with tactile sensory processing.

- ○ Scott will be provided with a quiet spot and a social story to teach him about the use of his quiet spot [see Figure 4.4, in Chapter 4]. He will also be provided with a picture card of the quiet spot.

- ○ Scott's teacher's aide will review the stress barometer with Scott when he appears to be stressed, and guide him through the relaxation strategies associated with it [see Figure 4.9, Chapter 4).

- ○ Scott's assistant will provide him with a stress ball to squeeze during stressful times of the day.

- ○ Scott will be assigned the last place in moving and waiting lines to avoid excess tactile stimulation.

- ○ Scott's desk will be placed on the end of a table arrangement in the classroom for the same reason as above.

- ○ Scott's social stories [see p.1 of this plan] will be used to introduce his rewards and consequences.

Hierarchy of consequential strategies to use when behavior occurs:

Reward system for good behavior:

- ○ Token system to earn airplane-related rewards: magazines, models, etc. [*see Figure 5.11, Chapter 5*].
- ○ Positive notes to student [*see Figure 5.13, Chapter 5*].
- ○ Notes to parents [*see Figure 5.12, Chapter 5*].

Methods and dates of data collection for evaluation:

CHAPTER SIX

Consequential Strategies

When teachers and parents look at what poor behavior may be communicating and work together to create meaningful antecedent strategies to address this behavior, consequential strategies take a 'back seat.' Indeed, many teachers report that often consequential strategies, although included in the behavior support plan, are used fairly infrequently when appropriate antecedent strategies are included in the plan. A behavioral support plan that utilizes many consequential strategies often is a plan that has not addressed the right hypothesis for the student or has not provided for enough antecedent strategies. When a child is experiencing more time in punishment situations than he/she is in academic learning situations, this too is a blatant indicator that he/she needs to have a behavioral support plan developed or revised. Typically, the more the inappropriate behavior increases, the more punishment is applied. In addition, the punishment usually becomes more severe. For this reason, intervening early, before the behavior has escalated, will allow teachers to use the minimum number of consequences at the least level of severity.

COMMUNICATING RULES

Teachers and parents need to communicate to students with autism the behaviors that are expected of them and in ways these children can understand. Children will need to know the rules and what will happen if they break these rules. Because children with autism are frequently visual or tactile learners, the rules need to be communicated to them in this manner, along with the consequences that will be applied if these rules are broken. Although communicating the rules is clearly an antecedent strategy, reviewing those rules once misbehavior has occurred can certainly be a consequential strategy as well. For younger children, pictures work well to communicate rules (Figure 6.1).

Social Story to Explain the Consequence of Hitting and Pushing

I am a good boy.

Sometimes I get mad at my friends and teachers.

They may do something that I do not like or makes me upset.

When I am upset, I must not hit other people.

I must not push other people.

Hitting and pushing is not allowed. These are school rules.

If I hit or push, I may hurt someone.

My teachers and parents will have to take away my computer time when I push or hit.

I can follow the rules and not hit and push.

Then, my friends will be happy and so will I.

I will enjoy my school day and so will my friends.

I will be able to use my computer and have fun.

Figure 6.1 Social story to explain the consequences of misbehavior

EXAMPLE I

Mrs Gregory's second-grade class had a written chart taped to the wall with the class rules. A boy with autism in her class frequently had trouble remembering those rules. His classroom aide developed a visual/tactile method to teach this boy the rules. She created a picture book with one written rule on each page. She asked the boy with autism to draw his own picture depicting the rule on each page. When he misbehaved and broke a rule, one of his consequences was to review the rulebook with his classroom aide. Mrs Gregory soon noticed that there were fewer occurrences of misbehavior after just two reviews of the rulebook.

When consequences are applied, they should be assigned a hierarchy from mild to severe, ranging from least intrusive to most intrusive. For instance, if redirection at the first sign of misbehavior would serve the purpose, it would not be appropriate to administer a restraint. If parents and teachers jump to the highest level of consequence at the first sign of occurrence, what will be done at the fourth and fifth occurrence? It is easy to see how behaviors could escalate and frustration could ensue without a methodical approach to addressing poor behavior. This is why it is critical that staff and parents need to agree to each consequence and establish a hierarchy that everyone can be comfortable with (see Scott Smith's behavioral support plan, Appendix 6.1).

Consistency in any behavior plan is important, especially for children with autism. If school handles certain behaviors one way and home handles them another, the child with autism who craves sameness and structure will experience much stress. This may actually result in even more inappropriate behaviors. Further, if one teacher follows the plan as written and another teacher does his/her own thing, this will also result in a plan that is inconsistent for the student with autism. Teamwork is essential for any behavior support plan to be successful.

As stated previously, it is essential that the hierarchy of consequences be explained to the student in a manner he will understand. Again, a visual or tactile manner works best (Figure 6.2).

The first time I hit or push today, I will lose my computer time for today.

The next time I hit or push today, I will have time out for 10 minutes.

The next time I hit or push today, I will have to go to the principal's office for the rest of the day and my parents will be called.

Figure 6.2 Hierarchy of Consequences for misbehavior

TYPES OF CONSEQUENCES

Teachers and parents frequently have used the following consequences to manage behavior:

- vocal reprimands ('no hitting!')

- writing the student's name on the board (embarrassment)

- loss of pleasurable activities (computer time, free time, assembly)

- in-school suspension (student is suspended from class for the remainder of the day or a succession of days)

- student is sent to the principal's office

- scare tactics ('You are going to fail my class!' or 'I'm going to call your parents!')

- verbal threats or warnings ('If you do that again, your seat will be moved!')

- in-classroom time out (away from the others in the class, but in the same classroom)

- out-of-classroom time out (standing outside the classroom door).

Other types of strategies that could be effective and somewhat more positive in nature because they also ensure the student's understanding of his/her behavior include:

- having the student issue an apology with an explanation of what he/she did wrong ('I'm sorry that I ripped your paper')

- having the student explain, write or draw his/her depiction of what he/she did wrong

- reviewing the rule book or rule chart

- reviewing or developing a social story that explains the rule that was broken

- 'making up' for poor behavior (if he/she was unkind to another student, he/she would have to do something nice for him/her; if he/she is destructive with someone's property, he/she has to repair it)

In addition, the following have also been used effectively:

- points earned versus points lost program from Chapter 5

- ticket system – this works well for students who exhibit milder forms of poor behavior. The student is awarded a ticket each time he/she misbehaves. This method also serves as a communicating device to parents (Figure 6.3). A hierarchy is established with the tickets so that the student knows what consequence he/she will receive once he/she is awarded a certain number of tickets (Figure 6.4)

- time out by removing materials from the student (especially when he/she is being destructive)

- time out by having the student freeze on the spot.

This Ticket is Issued for:

1.   Not doing my homework.
2.   Not finishing my classwork.
3.   Not being respectful to my teacher.
4.   Not being kind to my classmates.
5.   Not paying attention in class.

Figure 6.3 Ticket system for misbehavior

Fines for Tickets

One ticket:	Warning from the teacher.
Two tickets:	Review the rules.
Three tickets:	Loss of computer time.
Four tickets:	Ten-minute time out.
Five tickets:	Seat is moved to the back of the room for the rest of the day.
Six tickets:	Principal's office for rest of day and parents are called.

Figure 6.4 Fine system for receiving tickets

IMPORTANT POINTS ABOUT THE USE OF TIME OUTS

This author once observed a regular education classroom where a disabled student's desk was in permanent time out, away from his classmates in a far back corner. Apparently, his behaviors had gotten to the point where he was required to sit in his regular education classroom for the entire school day at a study corral (a type of desk with high sides that makes it impossible for the student to look out over them unless he stands up). The student's teachers were happy that his behavior was now under control and that he could not bother anyone around him. Because his behavior improved so dramatically, they associated this consequence with success. The author could not see how inclusion was being accomplished at this point for the child and saw this as a permanent-type consequence, since no formal behavior assessment had been completed to determine why he was misbehaving.

This is a classic example of the result of not addressing the behavior when it was more manageable. The child's disappointed parent suggested that maybe he could be offered the reward of sitting at a regular desk for a while if his behavior was good during a certain time frame. How sad that some schools are now rewarding students with inclusion when they behave. The following points need to be considered with regards to time out:

1. Choose a nonstimulating room or area for the time out. The student will not want to be there very long if he/she has nothing to read, look at or listen to while he/she is there.

2. Use a kitchen timer to set the length of time out for the student. Timers are 'neutral.' If the teacher uses his/her watch to determine the length of the time out, the student may feel that the teacher is deliberately keeping him/her in time out longer than the time allotted. For the student, the minutes pass by very slowly in time out.

3. Apply one minute of time out for each year of the student's age.

4. No one should talk to or make contact with the student while he/she is in time out unless he/she is in physical danger.

5. When the student leaves the time out, he/she should be able to explain, draw or write the reason why he/she was put there. If the student can't, this needs to be explained to him/her in a way that he/she will understand (social story, rulebook, picture, etc.). No additional lecturing should be given when time out is over. The student has completed his/her punishment. The teacher should adopt a welcoming

attitude and at once include him/her back in the classroom activities.

6. If the student resists the use of time out, he/she should be awarded an extra minute in time out.

7. Flick (1996, p.77) states that the use of time out should be rehearsed with the student beforehand. For instance, you could say, 'If you hit or kick someone again today, you will sit here [show him the place] for time out for ten minutes. I will set the timer to keep track of the time. I will not speak to you, and you cannot speak to me while you are in time out. When the timer rings, you can leave the area and return to your regular seat; however, you will have to tell me first what you did wrong. If you don't know the reason you were in time out, I will tell you. If you argue with me about going to time out, I will add one extra minute onto your time. Do you understand?' Again, this will work better for students with autism if time out is explained in a visual form. If the student is destructive in time out, at the end of his/her time out, he/she will need to clean up his/her mess before he/she can come out. Time out should only be used for those behaviors which are of the acting out type or aggressive, including the following:

    • hitting, biting, kicking, throwing, scratching, pinching, pushing, or mistreating others and/or objects

    • temper tantrums

    • name calling and/or mean teasing

    • back talking

    • cursing.

The following types of behaviors are usually not effective or appropriate for time out:

- not completing classwork/homework

- inattentiveness

- forgetting classwork/homework/school supplies or other organization skill problems

- sensory processing difficulties (a separate area or 'safe spot' should be used for these problems)

- stress and anxiety due to lack of modifications to environment

- behaviors which arise from issues of self-esteem or depression

- academic deficits

- behaviors arising because of transition difficulties due to lack of modifications to the environment

- social problems arising from the student's inability to understand and function appropriately as typical children do.

The author would like to close this chapter by adding that as a teacher, there are certain behaviors that are never acceptable in the school environment (violent and/or aggressive type behaviors). They cannot be tolerated for any reason. However, children with autism have a disability that spans many areas: social, language, behavioral, sensory, cognitive. We must be sure that we are looking at the child's deficits and helping him/her to learn appropriate ways of behaving in the school environment before we begin to administer serious punishments or consequences. We cannot assume that these children know the rules or are at a developmental age where they should no longer be displaying certain behaviors. Nothing can be assumed with children with autism. A good rule of thumb to apply is that for every consequence in a behavioral support plan, there should be at least three antecedent strategies used to address the *teaching* or the *environmental supports* that the student will need to be able to exhibit positive behavior.

APPENDIX 6.1

Behavioral Support Plan, page 1

Student name: Scott Smith   **Date:**   February 5, 2002

Define the problem behavior and why it is important to change:

Scott is exhibiting aggression with peers and staff. He is also having crying spells and periods where he yells out.

Hypothesis regarding the problem behavior:

Scott is experiencing some academic skill deficits in reading class and deficits in his fine motor skills in art class.

Identified skill to be taught to reduce problem behavior:

Scott will need to improve his fourth-grade reading skills (especially in comprehension) with the help of his learning support and classroom teacher. He will need additional occupational therapy and practice to develop his fine motor skills in the area of cutting, pasting and handling small items.

Antecedent strategies to put in place to prevent behavior:

- Scott will attend learning support for reading each day for the second half of reading.

- Scott will place his pencil horizontally on his desk to cue his teacher when he needs help.

- Scott will be provided with modified worksheets and tests, and directions will be written in the form of a checklist for Scott. His parents will be given blank story maps to use at home.

- Scott will receive additional occupational therapy, and his parents will be given exercises to use with Scott at home.

- Scott will be given a social story about aggression and this will be reviewed with Scott so that he can know what his consequences will be when he is aggressive [*see Figure 6.1, Chapter 6*].

- Scott will be provided with a social story to explain his reward system [*see Figure 5.11, Chapter 5*].

Hierarchy of consequential strategies to use when behavior occurs:

- ○ Scott's team will use the ticket system and follow the order of consequences on the ticket [*see Figure 6.4, Chapter 6*].
- ○ The team will devise a picture story to explain the order of consequences (*see example Figure 6.2, Chapter 6*).

Reward system for good behavior:

- ○ Token system to earn airplane-related rewards: magazines, models, etc. [*see Figure 5.11, Chapter 5*].
- ○ Positive notes to student [*see Figure 5.13, Chapter 5*).
- ○ Notes to parents [*see Figure 5.12, Chapter 5*).

Methods and dates of data collection for evaluation:

Behavioral Support Plan, Page 2

Student name: Scott Smith   **Date:**   February 5, 2001

Define the problem behavior and why it is important to change:

Scott is exhibiting aggression with peers and staff. He is also having crying spells and periods where he yells out.

Hypothesis regarding the problem behavior:

Scott is having problems with transitions.

Identified skill to be taught to reduce problem behavior:

Scott will move through the daily changes in his school schedule without crying or becoming upset.

Antecedent strategies to put in place to prevent behavior:

- ○ Scott will be provided each day with a picture schedule of his daily schedule. His teacher assistant will review it with him each day. He will also have changes alerted to him as soon as they become available.

- ○ Scott will be given five-minute warnings before transitions are about to take place by his teacher or teacher's aide, and his picture schedule will be reviewed with him.

- ○ If Scott seems to be having a particularly stressful day, his teacher assistant will move Scott through his transition before the other children (i.e. take him to his other classes one minute earlier).

- ○ Scott's social stories [see p.1 of this plan] will be used to introduce his rewards and consequences.

Hierarchy of consequential strategies to use when behavior occurs:

- ○ Scott's team will use the ticket system and follow the order of consequences on the ticket [see Figure 6.4, Chapter 6].

- ○ The team will devise a picture story to explain the order of consequences [see example Figure 6.2, Chapter 6].

Reward system for good behavior:

○ Token system to earn airplane-related rewards: magazines, models, etc. [*see Figure 5.11, Chapter 5*].

○ Positive notes to student [*see Figure 5.13, Chapter 5*].

○ Notes to parents [*see Figure 5.12, Chapter 5*).

Methods and dates of data collection for evaluation:

Behavioral Support Plan, page 3

Student name: Scott Smith   **Date:**   February 5, 2002

Define the problem behavior and why it is important to change:

Scott is exhibiting aggression with peers and staff. He is also having crying spells and periods where he yells out.

Hypothesis regarding the problem behavior:

Scott is having sensory integration problems, especially tactile defensiveness.

Identified skill to be taught to reduce problem behavior:

Scott will be able to stay calm and not overreact when he is touched or when people invade his space.

Antecedent strategies to put in place to prevent behavior:

- Scott's occupational therapist will focus on some activities to help with tactile sensory processing.

- Scott will be provided with a quiet spot and a social story to teach him about the use of his quiet spot [see Figure 4.4, Chapter Four]. He will also be provided with a picture card of the quiet spot.

- Scott's teacher's aide will review the stress barometer with Scott when he appears to be stressed, and guide him through the relaxation strategies associated with it [see Figure 4.9, Chapter 4].

- Scott's assistant will provide him with a stress ball to squeeze during stressful times of the day.

- Scott will be assigned the last place in moving and waiting lines to avoid excess tactile stimulation.

- Scott's desk will be placed on the end of a table arrangement in the classroom for the same reason as above.

- Scott's social stories [see p.1 of this plan] will be used to introduce his rewards and consequences.

Hierarchy of consequential strategies to use when behavior occurs:

- ○ Scott's team will use the ticket system and follow the order of consequences on the ticket [*see Figure 6.4, Chapter 6*].
- ○ The team will devise a picture story to explain the order of consequences [*see example Figure 6.2, Chapter 6*].

Reward system for good behavior:

- ○ Token system to earn airplane-related rewards: magazines, models, etc. [*see Figure 5.11, Chapter 5*].
- ○ Positive notes to student [*see Figure 5.13, Chapter 5*]
- ○ Notes to parents [*see Figure 5.12, Chapter 5*].

Methods and dates of data collection for evaluation:

CHAPTER SEVEN

Evaluation for Effectiveness

As stated previously, it is critical that the plan be developed as a team, and that each team member can share input, voice concerns and understand his/her role so that consistency for the student can be achieved. All team members then have to agree to the plan's contents and be comfortable adopting it. The only way, however, to determine if the plan is successful is for each team member to keep data to see if the number of problem behaviors that were addressed are increasing, decreasing or staying the same. (See Scott Smith's behavior support plan and the 'methods and dates of evaluation' section in Appendix 7.1.)

EVALUATING FOR EFFECTIVENESS

Hopefully, at this point in time, baseline data from the initial two-week observations (see Chapter 2) has already been collected. By reviewing those observations and graphing the behavior, we should be able to determine the frequency of our problem behaviors across the same two-week span (Figure 7.1). The clock-time of the behaviors can also be depicted in graph form for team members for each observation day. This will make it easier for participants to see the time periods/subject areas where the student is having difficulty.

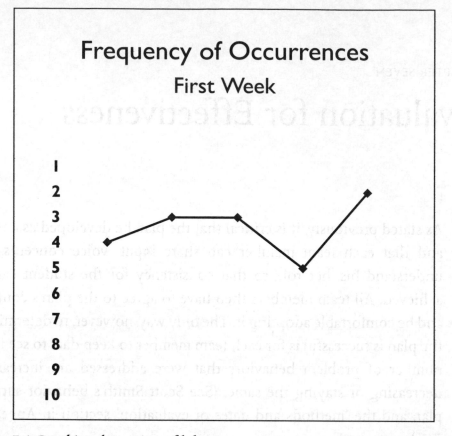

Figure 7.1 Graphing observations of behavior

Once the new plan goes into effect, however, we should also keep data for at least the same amount of time to compare frequency of occurrences of problem behavior with those kept during our initial observation period. A decreasing number of occurrences indicate(s) that the behavioral support plan is working, and the student is learning new skills to avoid using negative behavior as a form of communication.

If the number of behaviors have increased or stayed the same, there could be several reasons why. Perhaps the plan has not addressed the right hypothesis, the antecedent strategies that have been put in place are not effective, or the reward system may not be a strong motivator for the student.

EXAMPLE I
Larry's behavioral support plan was put into place three weeks ago. The team has kept careful data and determined that his behaviors have not improved at all. One of the reinforcers chosen for Larry was a sticker system. His classroom aide was not present during the development of the plan due to illness, but attended the session where the team was considering what changes needed to be made to help reduce the number of problem behaviors. She shared with the team that Larry was tactile defensive. He despised stickers because of the sticky residue they left behind when removed. He would frequently try to remove them from his papers, and he would get aggravated when his papers were returned from his teacher with stickers. She felt that this motivator was not appropriate for Larry. The team removed the stickers as rewards and adopted a token system. Then they took data for another week. The number of behaviors Larry displayed decreased dramatically, as he was now able to accumulate tokens to earn a reward that was more meaningful to him.

A program's effectiveness can also be evaluated by determining if there has been an increase in skills that the student was lacking (stress management techniques, better academic skills, social behavior skills, etc.) Identifying the particular skill that needs to be taught to the student in the behavioral support plan document is the way that teachers and parents can ensure that the behaviors won't reoccur. If the student has mastered this skill, he/she will no longer need to communicate his/her frustration through poor behavior. The identified skill to be taught in the behavioral support plan can also be measured:

EXAMPLE II
Joshua had a low threshold for frustration. He would frequently react with angry outbursts whenever he experienced even mild forms of stress. Joshua's behavioral support plan team determined that Joshua's identified skill to be taught should be stress management. After his behavioral support plan went into effect, Joshua was taught various ways to cope with his stress using antecedent strategies (such as those found in Chapter 4) designed especially for him. Today, Joshua can

frequently demonstrate appropriate ways of handling stress. He no longer has outbursts because he can recognize when he is approaching his threshold. He then requests some quiet time so that he can 'regroup.'

The team should implement the plan for at least two weeks to determine its effectiveness, and then meet immediately to revise it if the data collected shows that it is not working. It is not appropriate to discard the plan and declare all the valuable observation data useless without first examining each of the plan's areas (hypothesis, identified skill to be taught, antecedent strategies, consequences, motivators) to determine if one or more should be modified or improved.

MAKING REVISIONS TO THE BEHAVIORAL SUPPORT PLAN

Too often parents and teachers assume that because a behavior plan is working, it has 'done the trick' and can be phased out. Properly developed behavioral support plans don't 'fix' problem behavior – they help to provide the supports to the student so that he/she can learn the skills necessary to avoid such behavior. If the antecedent strategies are withdrawn too soon or the rewards and consequential strategies are not applied consistently, the student may lose the motivation to continue his/her learning and the behaviors will return.

There will often be relapses in problem behavior if supports are withdrawn or if new stimuli are presented (i.e. substitute teacher, new classroom, new schedule, etc.) Supports should be kept in place for students with autism because of their need for consistency and sameness. In addition, supports may need to be adapted or modified as the need arises.

EXAMPLE I
Mrs Strong, the fourth-grade teacher of Ross, a child with autism, was scheduled for maternity leave in three weeks. Mr Lynch was hired to

replace her for the remainder of the school year. Because of Ross's problematic behavior, Mrs Strong instructed Mr Lynch in all parts of Ross's behavioral support plan. In addition, she introduced Mr Lynch to Ross and provided Ross with the added supports of a social story and a calendar indicating when the transition would occur.

EXAMPLE II

Michael's behavioral support plan was working wonderfully for the two behaviors (aggression and work refusal) that the team was addressing. However, he still had problems with inappropriate behavior during recess and other unstructured times of the day. The team later agreed that it was necessary to add another system of support using a 'lunch buddy' program where Michael could learn social language and social behavior skills in small groups with typical peers. This small group instruction time would help Michael to learn new social skills so that he could interact better with peers during his recess and lunch periods.

EXAMPLE III

In Jennifer's behavioral support plan, the team identified that her language processing ability was significantly behind that of her peers. As she moved on through the elementary grades, this gap widened even more. It became very apparent in third grade, when her behaviors returned, that she needed additional supports. She struggled to understand and follow directions, and her grades were poor. The team agreed to provide her with visual supports in this area and to increase her speech and language classes from once a week to twice. They also decided that if Jennifer was still very frustrated in her current placement by the end of the school year they may need to consider an alternative placement for next school year.

There are times, of course, when the behavioral support plan may be ineffective. The number of problem behaviors may not change, or may actually increase. As stated previously, a common reason for this is that the plan has not addressed the correct hypothesis for the behavior. In addition, another common mistake is made when the antecedent strategies do not address the behavior until after it has occurred, rather than helping to prevent its occurrence. Thus, they are really *consequential strategies*.

> EXAMPLE I
>
> Mary's behavior was identified by her team as stemming from a lack of consistency in receiving consequences. Her antecedent strategies included such things as 'verbal prompts when she is becoming too loud' or 'removal from the room to discuss her behavior.' In actuality, these were not antecedents, they were *consequences*, because they were used *after* the behavior occurred and not before. As a result, Mary's behavioral support plan consisted of nothing more than a list of consequences she would receive when she was too loud and the plan was not effective.

When a behavioral support plan has been developed over several weeks and is determined not to be effective at all in addressing problem behaviors, the team and the student will certainly be very frustrated. At such times it may be useful that someone with autism expertise begin to observe the child and make recommendations, as an accurate 'diagnosis' of the problem will be essential to reduce this frustration level.

WEANING REWARDS AWAY FROM THE STUDENT

Teachers and parents frequently ask when it is appropriate to wean the student from his/her reward system. The author feels that it is never appropriate to withdraw all rewards for good behavior. However, tangible rewards can gradually be reduced from a more formal method (such as the marble or token method in Chapter 5) to a less formal method (praise and occasional tangible rewards). It is important that the student be taken to this stage slowly so that he/she will not feel cheated out of his/her reward system and still be motivated to behave appropriately. Grad Flick notes:

If [you] become lax and return to earlier, unsuccessful ways of dealing with behavior (e.g. using critical comments), then the alternative to the desirable behavior may again surface....When you get improvement (i.e., more desirable behavior), you maintain it with periodic reinforcement (i.e., praise or other rewards). (Flick 1996, p.xxi)

In summary, the most effective behavioral support plans include the following:

- a team approach where all staff who interact with the student have input and opportunity to share ideas and concerns about the student and his/her behaviors

- a thorough observation of problem behavior to determine its *communicative intent*

- the identification of from one to three target behaviors that the plan should address

- the identification of one to three target skills (one for each target behavior above) that the student needs to be taught so that he/she can avoid choosing inappropriate behavior as a means of communication

- an array of antecedent strategies designed to teach the student the identified skill or to lend support before the problem behavior occurs so that hopefully the student will no longer have the need to use the behaviors

- the selection of a meaningful motivator *for the student* that will be effective in helping to reduce the target behaviors

- clear and concise consequential strategies arranged in a hierarchy form that are positive in nature

- an established method of collecting data to measure the success of the behavioral support plan

- a willingness on the part of the team to persevere and to modify or change the plan as the need arises.

Children with autism represent a significant sector of the student special education population today. Their need for supports are great, and these supports may or may not be typical of those that other special education students require. As educators and parents, we must sometimes be flexible and willing to look at many alternative methods to achieve success with these students. Too often, when we do not understand the child's disability and how it may impact on his/her behavior, problem behaviors are not identified as manifestations of his/her disability when they really are. The student is then assigned the same disciplinary procedures that are applicable to typical students, and the number and type of behaviors escalate. A behavioral support plan is not the same thing as a discipline plan. It does not focus merely on what punishments the child will receive when his/her behavior is inappropriate. It is a document that provides for an array of positive supports for the student with autism. These supports offer the assurance that inclusion of a child with autism in the regular education classroom can be successful.

APPENDIX 7.1

Behavioral Support Plan, page 1

Student name: Scott Smith   **Date:**   February 5, 2002

Define the problem behavior and why it is important to change:

Scott is exhibiting aggression with peers and staff. He is also having crying spells and periods where he yells out.

Hypothesis regarding the problem behavior:

Scott is experiencing some academic skill deficits in reading class and deficits in his fine motor skills in art class.

Identified skill to be taught to reduce problem behavior:

Scott will need to improve his fourth-grade reading skills (especially in comprehension) with the help of his learning support and classroom teacher. He will need additional occupational therapy and practice to develop his fine motor skills in the area of cutting, pasting and handling small items.

Antecedent strategies to put in place to prevent behavior:

- Scott will attend learning support for reading each day for the second half of reading.
- Scott will place his pencil horizontally on his desk to cue his teacher when he needs help.
- Scott will be provided with modified worksheets and tests, and directions will be written in the form of a checklist for Scott. His parents will be given blank story maps to use at home.
- Scott will receive additional occupational therapy, and his parents will be given exercises to use with Scott at home.
- Scott will be given a social story about aggression and this will be reviewed with Scott so that he can know what his consequences will be when he is aggressive [*see Figure 6.1, Chapter 6*].
- Scott will be provided with a social story to explain his reward system [*see Figure 5.11, Chapter 5*].

Hierarchy of consequential strategies to use when behavior occurs:

○ Scott's team will use the ticket system and follow the order of consequences on the ticket [*see Figure 6.4, Chapter 6*].

○ The team will devise a picture story to explain the order of consequences [*see example Figure 6.2, Chapter 6*).

Reward system for good behavior:

○ Token system to earn airplane-related rewards: magazines, models, etc. [*see Figure 5.11, Chapter 5*).

○ Positive notes to student [*see Figure 5.13, Chapter 5*].

○ Notes to parents [*see Figure 5.12, Chapter 5*].

Methods and dates of data collection for evaluation:

A standardized reading test will be administered at the start of this plan and repeated in six months to see if Scott has improved in this area. Also, an occupational therapy evaluation will be administered at the start of this plan and again in six months to see if there is improvement in fine motor ability.

Behavioral Support Plan, page 2

Student name: Scott Smith   **Date:**   February 5, 2002

Define the problem behavior and why it is important to change:

Scott is exhibiting aggression with peers and staff. He is also having crying spells and periods where he yells out.

Hypothesis regarding the problem behavior:

Scott is having problems with transitions.

Identified skill to be taught to reduce problem behavior:

Scott will move through the daily changes in his school schedule without crying or becoming upset.

Antecedent strategies to put in place to prevent behavior:

- Scott will be provided each day with a picture schedule of his daily schedule. His teacher assistant will review it with him each day. He will also have changes alerted to him as soon as they become available.

- Scott will be given five-minute warnings before transitions are about to take place by his teacher or teacher's aide, and his picture schedule will be reviewed with him.

- If Scott seems to be having a particularly stressful day, his teacher assistant will move Scott through his transition before the other children (i.e. take him to his other classes one minute earlier).

- Scott's social stories [see p.1 of this plan] will be used to introduce his rewards and consequences.

Hierarchy of consequential strategies to use when behavior occurs:

- Scott's team will use the ticket system and follow the order of consequences on the ticket [see Figure 6.4, Chapter 6].

- The team will devise a picture story to explain the order of consequences [see example Figure 6.2, Chapter 6].

Reward system for good behavior:

- ○ Token system to earn airplane-related rewards: magazines, models, etc. [*see Figure 5.11, Chapter 5*].
- ○ Positive notes to student [*see Figure 5.13, Chapter 5*].
- ○ Notes to parents [*see Figure 5.12, Chapter 5*].

Methods and dates of data collection for evaluation:

Data will be collected daily for two weeks beginning February 6, 2002 using a frequency of occurrence chart.

Behavioral Support Plan, page 3

Student name: Scott Smith   Date: February 5, 2002

Define the problem behavior and why it is important to change:

Scott is exhibiting aggression with peers and staff. He is also having crying spells and periods where he yells out.

Hypothesis regarding the problem behavior:

Scott is having sensory integration problems, especially tactile defensiveness.

Identified skill to be taught to reduce problem behavior:

Scott will be able to stay calm and not overreact when he is touched or when people invade his space.

Antecedent strategies to put in place to prevent behavior:

○ Scott's occupational therapist will focus on some activities to help with tactile sensory processing.

○ Scott will be provided with a quiet spot and a social story to teach him about the use of his quiet spot (*see Figure 4.4, Chapter 4*). He will also be provided with a picture card of the quiet spot.

○ Scott's teacher's aide will review the stress barometer with Scott when he appears to be stressed, and guide him through the relaxation strategies associated with it [*see Figure 4.9, Chapter 4*].

○ Scott's assistant will provide him with a stress ball to squeeze during stressful times of the day.

○ Scott will be assigned the last place in moving and waiting lines to avoid excess tactile stimulation.

○ Scott's desk will be placed on the end of a table arrangement in the classroom for the same reason as above.

○ Scott's social stories [*see p.1 of this plan*] will be used to introduce his rewards and consequences.

Hierarchy of consequential strategies to use when behavior occurs:

- ○ Scott's team will use the ticket system and follow the order of consequences on the ticket [*see Figure 6.4, Chapter 6*].
- ○ The team will devise a picture story to explain the order of consequences [*see example Figure 6.2, Chapter 6.*].

Reward system for good behavior:

- ○ Token system to earn airplane-related rewards: magazines, models, etc. [*see Figure 5.11, Chapter 5*].
- ○ Positive notes to student [*see Figure 5.13, Chapter 5*].
- ○ Notes to parents [*see Figure 5.12, Chapter 5*].

Methods and dates of data collection for evaluation:

Data will be collected daily for two weeks beginning February 6, 2002 using a frequency of occurrence chart.

References

Ayers, A. J. (1989) 'Sensory integration and praxis tests.' Los Angeles: Western Psychological Services.

Baron-Cohen, S. (2001) 'The core deficts of autism and disorders of relating and communication.' Special edition of *Journal of Developmental and Learning Disorders 5*, 1, 47–75.

Flick, G. (1996) *Power Parenting for Children with ADD/ADHD – A Practical Parent's Guide for Managing Difficult Behaviors*. West Nyack, NY: Center for Applied Research Education Simon and Schuster Company.

Goleman, D. (1995) *Emotional Intelligence – Why it Can Matter More Than IQ.* New York: Bantam Books.

Grandin, T. (1995) *Thinking in Pictures and Other Reports from My Life with Autism*. New York: Doubleday.

Gray, C. (1994a) *Comic Strip Conversations*. Arlington, TX: Future Horizons.

Gray, C. (1994b) *The Original Social Story Book*. Arlington, TX: Future Horizons.

Hodgdon, L. (1995) 'Solving Social-Behavioural Problems Through the Use of Visually Supported Communication.' In K.A. Quill *Teaching Children with Autism – Strategies to Enhance Communication and Socialization*. New York: Delmar.

Kauffman, J. (1999) 'How we prevent the prevention of emotional and behavioral disorders.' *Exceptional Children 65*, 4, 448–468.

Moyes, R. (2001) *Incorporating Social Goals in the Classroom – A Guide for Teachers and Parents of Children with High-Functioning Autism and Aspergers' Syndrome*. London: Jessica Kingsley Publishers.

Prizant, B. M. and Duchan, J. F. (1981) 'The functions of immediate echolalia in autistic children.' *Journal of Speech and Hearing Disorders 46*, 241–249.

Rehabilitation Act, Section 504. Published at 29 U.S.C. Section 794 and the implementing regulations at 34 C.F.R. Part 104.

Wantuch, T. (2001) 'A summer social skills program.' Mason, Ohio: emerge7799@netzero.net.

References

Index